MEDIEVAL POOR LAW

MEDIEVAL POOR LAW

A Sketch of Canonical Theory
and Its Application in England

BY BRIAN TIERNEY

UNIVERSITY OF CALIFORNIA PRESS

Berkeley and Los Angeles   1959

University of California Press
Berkeley and Los Angeles, California
Cambridge University Press, London, England

© 1959 BY THE REGENTS OF THE UNIVERSITY OF CALIFORNIA

PUBLISHED WITH THE ASSISTANCE OF A
GRANT FROM THE FORD FOUNDATION

Library of Congress Catalog Card No. 59-5148

Designed by Marion Jackson Skinner

To
Richard O'Dowd

Foreword

In this stimulating book Brian Tierney has added nearly five centuries to the documented history of the social services. He has erected a new bench mark for social workers and students of the social sciences to use in measuring and appraising the development of public assistance.

This book is an expansion and enrichment of four lectures delivered in January, 1956, at the School of Social Welfare of the University of California, Los Angeles. Professor Tierney, an authority on ecclesiastical jurisprudence, has here brought together from a variety of materials the significant concepts and principles upon which the Middle Ages drew in dealing with the problem of poverty and the relief of need. This work has involved not only the study of the Decretum of Gratian—a compilation of papal decrees, canons of Church councils, and commentaries and opinions of the Church Fathers—first issued in 1140, but also the study of the commentaries of later canonists and the great corpus of documents concerning the Church's legislation, actions, and attitudes toward the evolution of a system of public assistance.

As Professor Tierney explains, the Church was a government, paralleling the secular government. The Church made laws, enforced and administered them, levied taxes, maintained courts, and was the essential legal authority in many areas of life. Indeed, in studying the history of social services we can now begin with the twelfth century instead of with the famous poor law of 1601, in the forty-third year of the reign of Elizabeth I.

The framework of discussion and argument within which Professor Tierney writes will be familiar to medievalists; it will be less so to most of us in the social welfare field. Professor Tierney has, to an unusual degree, the faculty of being interesting and, as the reader moves through the twelfth and the succeeding three centuries, he will find a relevance for our own generation in many of the conclusions of the canonists of the Middle Ages.

This book will, I am certain, enlarge the perspective of social workers and indeed be read with profit and enjoyment by students of law, of Church history, and by all persons interested in knowing something of the ideas which today form part of our culture.

KARL DE SCHWEINITZ
School of Social Welfare
University of California, Los Angeles

Preface

The great revival in canonistic studies during the past twenty years, made possible in large part by the labors of Dr. Stephan Kuttner on the unedited source material, has attracted the attention of scholars who are not specialists in legal history principally through the numerous stimulating works on medieval political thought which it has inspired. One purpose of this little book is to indicate the potentialities of canonistic research in another sphere, where the legal sources have been much less exploited and which may also be of interest to medievalists generally. This is the sphere of medieval social thought and social action. The topic selected, *Medieval Poor Law*, seems at first glance a limited one; but in fact any attempt to deal with it comprehensively involves a consideration of the whole structure of medieval society and the whole complex of medieval ecclesiastical institutions. It is a common experience in this kind of research; one plucks at some strand of doctrine and a whole skein of tangled and interdependent theories begins to unwind. Hence, although I have presented my own views clearly enough (I hope), a preliminary survey of this kind, in a field where much monographic research remains to be done, is necessarily more concerned to identify the problems that need investigation than to insist on definitive solutions to them.

The lectures on which the book is based were originally delivered

to an audience of social workers in the School of Social Welfare of
the University of California, Los Angeles. They therefore contained explanatory material relating to the position of the Church
in medieval society and the structure of church law which would
have been uncalled for in an exposition addressed solely to medievalists. It also seemed appropriate at certain points to explain medieval
ideas by comparing them with more recent ones which are familiar
to social work students. I have allowed some of this material to
stand in this revised version of the lectures in the hope that the
book may be of use to social workers interested in the historical
background of their profession, as well as to students of medieval
law and social theory. Again, since the book is not intended only
for medieval specialists, quotations from the sources included in
the lectures are presented in translation. In the notes it has seemed
reasonable to give the original Latin when the sense of the passage
is clearly conveyed in the accompanying English text.

I have to thank above all Professor Karl de Schweinitz for much
helpful advice and criticism based on his lifelong experience in the
fields of social welfare administration and teaching. I am grateful
too to Dean Donald S. Howard of the School of Social Welfare at
the University of California, Los Angeles, for his interest and en-
couragement. Finally, it is a pleasure to express my gratitude to
the John Simon Guggenheim Memorial Foundation, whose generous grants made possible the research on which this book is based.

BRIAN TIERNEY

CONTENTS

CHAPTER

1 *Poverty*

To the modern social worker it may well seem that medieval
canon law is an obscure and esoteric field of investigation, remote
from his own problems and preoccupations. In recent years, however, historians have become more and more impressed by the
value of the canonists' writings as source material for the study
of medieval civilization, especially in the realms of political thought
and economic theory. The canonistic works are particularly valuable in the study of poor law history, for an investigation of them
can introduce us to a whole system of jurisprudence which dealt
in detailed fashion with topics like the legal status of the poor, the
nature of their claims on individuals and on society, and the administration of the institutions through which relief was distributed.

The results of such an investigation may be interesting from
several points of view. The student who approaches the history
of poor relief from a background of social work is likely to find
himself mainly concerned with the development of contemporary
attitudes by evolution from or reaction against those of the recent
past, and with the immediate origins of the modern social work
profession among the pioneers of the nineteenth century. For him
a study of the medieval canonists presents an opportunity for another kind of historical thinking, for a comparative study of the
divergences and resemblances between the assumptions underly-

ing modern systems of poor relief and those of an earlier civilization whose jurists also reflected in sophisticated fashion on the
problems of poverty. For the economic historian the study of
medieval poor law may provide some fresh material relevant to
the continuing and tangled debate over the interaction of religious
and economic ideas in the transition from the Middle Ages to the
modern world; and the legal historian can find in this field some
particularly interesting exemplifications of one of the central themes
of jurisprudence, the perennial interplay of law and ethics.

Church law is extremely important for understanding medieval
attitudes to social questions simply because the Church itself was
extremely important in every sphere of medieval social life. The
position of the Church in medieval Europe was quite different
from that of the churches in modern America, and if we seek to
describe its status and functions we are launched at once into a
world of ideas and institutions significantly different from our own,
which may indeed seem repugnant to some types of modern religious sensibility, but which was accepted as entirely normal and
proper for several hundred years by sages and saints as well as
by fools and knaves. It will perhaps be useful, therefore, to consider the position of the Church in medieval society and the structure of ecclesiastical law before turning to specific problems of
poor relief. Incidentally, the law with which we shall be dealing
was intended to apply over the whole of Christendom, but, for
the sake of coherence, it has seemed best to take the examples
of its practical workings from one province of the Church. I have
chosen England because the English poor law tradition will probably seem to have most relevance for American society. For the
same reasons, in comparing medieval ideas with later ones, I shall
again refer mainly to English experience and English law.

We tend to think of churches as private voluntary institutions
within the state. The state is the public authority that acts on
behalf of us all, to which we all owe allegiance. The state makes
laws and its legislation binds us all. It levies taxes and we all have
to pay. It has law courts and prisons to enforce its commands.
Churches, on the other hand, are voluntary societies which we join
or leave as we please, and whose rules and regulations we obey

or disobey according to our own consciences. We take it for granted that society is best organized when there is only one public authority, the state, which can impose laws on us all and enforce them with coercive sanctions.

Medieval men just as confidently took it for granted that, since man had a twofold destiny, a life of the body and a life of the spirit, a life to live here on earth and an eternal life in the hereafter, two public authorities were needed to promote the welfare of human society. There was what we call the state, the secular hierarchy of government, which concerned itself with temporal and mundane matters, and the Church, the ecclesiastical hierarchy of government, which concerned itself with spiritual and heavenly matters. There was only one Church in the Middle Ages and every one was a member of it except for a small minority of Jews and heretics, just as nowadays every one is a citizen of the state except for a small minority of resident aliens. The ecclesiastical government acted on behalf of all the people in spiritual matters as the secular government did in temporal matters. The Church made laws, and all were bound to obey. It levied taxes and all were obliged to pay. It had its own courts in which its laws were enforced, with sanctions ranging from trivial penances to imprisonment or excommunication. The rulers of the Church were not officers of a private society within the state; they were wielders of a public jurisdiction parallel to that of the secular rulers, and not derived from them. The organization of ecclesiastical government indeed transcended all state boundaries. The Church was an international society with an international center of government. The medieval Papacy was the only international government that has ever really worked in Europe since the days of the Roman Empire.

Some of what I describe is not peculiar to the Middle Ages. Catholics and many other Christians have always believed that, in founding his church, Christ did not merely leave an example for individuals to follow, but established an enduring community. Again, the Catholic Church has always tended to emphasize that, for the maintenance of unity and order in such a community, institutions of law and government are needed. The peculiar feature of the medieval polity was the allegiance of virtually the whole population of Western Europe to the one Church, and, arising from that and other historical factors, the extraordinary prestige of ecclesiastical institutions in those days. In these circumstances, not only was there a general acquiescence in the exercise of coercive jurisdiction by the Church, but also—and this is the point that especially concerns us—the Church was able to claim jurisdiction over many spheres of social life which nowadays would usually be regarded as the proper concern of the secular power. In principle church courts exercised jurisdiction over all ecclesiastical persons, all clerics, that is, and over all ecclesiastical cases. In practice the tendency of the canonists was to expand the latter term until it could include almost any sphere of social or economic life. Much of the petty litigation that came before church courts did indeed concern "ecclesiastical cases" in the narrower sense—legal suits over payment of church taxes or rights to church revenues, and prosecutions for offenses like assaults on the clergy, damage to church property, and breaches of the law concerning observance of Sundays and other holidays. As an example of the multifarious kinds of business that could come even under these headings we may cite the case of one Thomas Samson, who, in 1488, was indicted before the court of the Archdeacon of Canterbury for sailing out to loot a shipwreck. No one seems to have minded the looting; the point was that he did it on All Saints Day when he ought to have been in church, and so the powers of the archdeacon were properly invoked.[1]

There was much else besides. Marriage was a sacrament of the Church and so all questions relating to validity or nullity of marriages came before church courts, together with related questions touching legitimacy of children and disposal of marriage dowries. Again the church courts claimed jurisdiction over all cases involving oaths or vows, an important matter in the Middle Ages, and church courts dealt with all matters relating to probate of wills. Since the Church condemned usury, and since even nonusurious contracts involved solemn promises by the contractors, a whole range of commercial litigation came before church courts too. Thirteenth-century canonists even claimed that, to prevent

injustices, an ecclesiastical court could take cognizance of any
case whatsoever when the appropriate secular authority refused
to do justice in the matter. Finally, since the relief of the poor was
a precept of Christian charity, the Church most emphatically
claimed that the care and protection of the poor was a matter
pertaining to the ecclesiastical government, to be regulated by
ecclesiastical law.

These various claims were not always accepted without question
by the secular powers and there was indeed a good deal of friction.
In particular, the question of how far the Church could go in
protecting poor persons against alleged injustices in the secular
courts was a matter of some dispute. The jurisdictional aspect of
the medieval Church was summed up by one of the greatest of
legal historians, F. W. Maitland, who went so far as to say: "The
medieval church was a state. Convenience may forbid us to call
it a state very often, but we ought to do so from time to time,
for we could frame no acceptable definition of a state which would
not comprehend the church." [2] And he added that the Church
had laws, lawgivers, law courts, and lawyers. If I seem to be
laboring this point it is because it is central to the theme that
is to be developed. Canon law was the law of a universally acknowledged public authority, just as much true law as the law
of the state; and law relating to the relief of poverty was one
branch of canon law.

An investigation of the medieval law of poor relief, therefore,
must be concerned principally with the canon law books and the
writings of the canonists.[3] The fact that these writings have
hardly been used in this connection means that, whereas there are
many excellent histories of charity in general and of ecclesiastical
charities in particular,[4] no one has really attempted a study of
medieval poor *law*. The prevailing assumption seems to be that
the poor law, a system of poor relief regulated by a legal code
and administered by public authority, was in the main a development of the sixteenth century, anticipated only by occasional
statutes dating back to the fourteenth. In fact, the occasional
fragments of secular legislation that one comes upon in the medieval period, insofar as they related to the relief of poverty and

not to the suppression of vagrancy, were almost invariably mere reënactments of principles drawn from the canonistic works which contained the main body of medieval law in the field. In studying these works, therefore, we are exploring not only the prehistory of modern ecclesiastical charities but also the prehistory of modern public relief. Medieval canon law is no obscure eddy, outside the main stream of poor law history, but an important and neglected stretch of the main stream itself.

A sketch of the main features of this medieval poor law requires a few preliminary comments on the *Corpus Iuris Canonici* itself, and on the age that produced it, for some of the more important problems in the field arose from the actual structure of the canon law, which in turn was shaped by the historical process of its creation. The foundations were laid in the twelfth century, a time of brilliant new beginnings in many departments of life. There was a need then for new beginnings. After the Roman Empire crumbled away in the fifth and sixth centuries, the Western world endured a long age of chaos. It was a bleak and brutal time. There was no security or stability for peaceful folk; men willingly bargained away freedom for the protection of a lord; the sharpest argument was the edge of a sword. The Church shared in the general degradation. Nearly all ecclesiastical appointments and ecclesiastical revenues fell under the control of lay lords who commonly exploited them for their own economic advantage. By the tenth century the Papacy itself, become a prize of contending factions in Rome, had decayed to a state of squalid impotence.

But in the eleventh and twelfth centuries at last European society began to move out of the long winter of these Dark Ages into the springtime of a new civilization. It was as though Christendom bestirred itself after a long illness and put forth new energies in every sphere of activity. There was new literature, new art, new movements of reform in the Church. In architecture the somewhat stolid round vaults of the Romanesque gave way to the soaring pinnacles of the new Gothic style. In philosophy men began at last to grapple with the central problems of meta-physics and at last to bring the light of critical reason to bear on the ancient authorities which they had been quoting at one another for centuries past. Above all, there was a great revival of legal studies, associated especially with the rediscovery of the whole body of ancient Roman law as codified by Justinian. Men of the earlier Middle Ages had known as law only a rude muddle of feudal practice and Teutonic custom. The revived study of the Roman *Corpus*, in which the whole field of jurisprudence was systematically organized according to rational principles, came with the force of a revelation. There was no passion among medieval intellectuals stronger than the passion for order; in every sphere of life and thought they sought to substitute law for anarchy, to bring system out of the chaos they had inherited.

Now the law of the Church itself was in a thoroughly chaotic state at the beginning of the twelfth century. There was more than a thousand years' accumulation of heterogeneous material—decrees of popes, canons of local and general councils, opinions of revered church Fathers like Augustine and Jerome. The whole mass had never been adequately codified and it was full of internal contradictions. The great work of systematization was accomplished by Gratian, a monk of Bologna who, about 1140, produced the immensely influential work that became known as the *Decretum*. The *Decretum* was a systematic treatise on the law of the Church, arranged in dialectical form. Gratian's method was to state a problem, then cite all the authorities that he considered relevant for its solution. He first gave the texts that could be adduced in support of one side of the case, then those that favored the opposite side, and, finally, a summing up in which he set out his own opinion and explained how the apparently conflicting texts could be reconciled, or why one set was more acceptable than the other. (Gratian's own title for his work was *Concordia Discordantium Canonum.*)

The *Decretum* thus provided solutions for many outstanding problems, and an unmatched collection of legal texts. It had a phenomenal success and soon was adopted in all the law schools of Christendom as the standard "text" for the teaching of canon law. After its appearance, however, much new law for the whole church was promulgated by popes and general councils, and this was codified in subsequent volumes promulgated by authority of the Papacy. In 1234 came the *Decretals* of Pope Gregory IX. This was divided into five books, and the next volume, promulgated by Pope Boniface VIII in 1298, was known as the *Liber Sextus*, the sixth book. This was followed in 1317 by the Clementines, named after Pope Clement V. The Clementines formed the last officially promulgated volume of the *Corpus Iuris Canonici*, but unofficial collections of the decrees of later popes were made in works known as the *Extravagantes Joannis XXII* and the *Extravagantes Communes*.

All these volumes together constituted the medieval *Corpus Iuris Canonici*,[5] and around them there grow up a vast literature of treatises and glosses. In due time each volume acquired a commentary known as the *Glossa Ordinaria*—the Ordinary Gloss —which was normally used in the schools as the standard interpretation of the text.[6] These ordinary glosses are of especial importance for this inquiry because they reflect the currents of thought most commonly accepted among the canonists.

It is important to bear in mind that the later volumes of papally authorized decretals were not intended to supplant the *Decretum* of Gratian but to supplement it. The Decretals of 1234 were often referred to as the *Liber Extra*, the book "extra to," or "additional to," the *Decretum*, and the *Decretum* itself continued to be taught to budding canon lawyers all through the Middle Ages as the very foundation of their science. This is of particular interest here, for it happens that a large part of the law relating to poor relief is to be found in the *Decretum*. In this connection another point arises. There has been much learned discussion as to how far the texts assembled in the *Decretum* actually did have the force of law in the Middle Ages. It can be argued that only a sovereign legislator can make law. A text of, say, St. Ambrose or St. Augustine, mere private theologians after all, even though eminent ones, could not suddenly become legally binding on the whole Church simply because a twelfth-century monk put them in a legal textbook. This may be well enough in theory. But in actual practice, all through the Middle Ages, the texts of the *Decretum* were taught in the schools, appealed to in the courts, and cited in canonistic commentaries exactly as were the texts of the official volumes of decretals. Guido de Baysio, who produced a great commentary on the *Decretum* in 1300, explained at the beginning of his work that Gratian had assembled the canons of the Apostles and the decrees of councils and popes, and then, because these sources did not provide adequate discussion of all cases, had added texts of the holy Fathers "which today have the force of law." He was saying, in effect, that they had the force of law because Gratian had incorporated them in the *Decretum*.[7]

This situation illustrates the kind of problem that could arise from the structure of canon law itself. The texts on charity and poor relief which Gratian presented were often taken from works written in the early centuries of the Christian era, when the Church was establishing itself in the Roman Empire. But the whole structure of civil society was different then, and so too, in many ways, was the pattern of ecclesiastical organization. It is necessary to consider how far precepts derived from that different age were successfully assimilated by the canonists and adapted to the circumstances of their own times. Another interesting point in this connection, though it is more a matter for the technical legal historian and I shall touch only the fringes of it, is the use—and abuse—of Roman law principles by the canonists in their attempts to shape a coherent legal theory out of the fragments of patristic doctrine which Gratian presented. Again, the descriptions of ancient institutions which occur in the old texts of the *Decretum* must not be accepted uncritically as accurate descriptions of twelfth-century conditions. It is all too easy to stumble into naïve anachronistic blunders in dealing with Gratian's quotations.[8] Finally, a mere outline of legal theory cannot tell all there is to know about the care of the poor in the Middle Ages. Not every legal principle that is approved in theory is effectively enforced in practice, as contemporary experience indicates plainly enough. Or, to take a familiar example from the history of the poor law itself, the English reformers of 1834 envisaged the establishment of separate institutions for women, old people, and children, but in actual administrative practice, throughout the nineteenth century, all classes of paupers were herded together "in one demoralised mass of misery and vice," as the Webbs put it.

These reservations do not seriously detract from the great value
of canonistic sources in the study of medieval poor relief; they
only call for a certain wariness on the part of the investigator who
sets out to interpret those sources. An outline of legal theory does
not indeed reveal the whole truth. It provides only the bare
bones which must be filled out from the relatively abundant
material that is available concerning the practical conduct of
medieval charities. But without such an outline there seems no
basis for judging how far medieval practice conformed to medieval
principles, nor how far those principles themselves were sound
and humane. The bare bones of legal history may be dry and
hard, but a body without a skeleton is a somewhat flaccid affair;
and a good deal of writing on medieval poor relief seems to suffer
from that sort of flaccidity. The standard histories of charity
usually give a detailed account of the charitable practices of the
early Church and of the theories of the church Fathers; they
pass lightly over the Dark Ages with an occasional reference to
capitularies of Charlemagne and canons of local church councils;
then they consider in detail the organization of medieval charitable
institutions like hospitals and almshouses, and present some of
the theological speculations of the scholastic age, almost invariably
drawn from the works of St. Thomas Aquinas. All this is well
enough. But in the historical progression an important point
has been missed. To understand the content of medieval poor
law it is essential to know which of the early patristic precepts were
carried through the Dark Ages or were consciously revived, and
what elements of early church legislation were regarded as still
living law, authoritative and binding, in the high Middle Ages.
The question is not an empty one. On some disputable points two
or three different theories of charity could be deduced from the
works of the Fathers or the canons of early councils by an appropriate selection of texts. The important thing is to know which
ones Gratian did select and accept, which ones "obtained the force
of law" through their incorporation in the *Decretum*. Again, when
Gratian himself presented conflicting texts on points of poor law,
as he often did, it is important to know what line the canonists
took in interpreting them, and to know, too, how effectively the

medieval popes supplemented the old law of the *Decretum* with
new legislation.

Since we are dealing with lawyers, perhaps the best first approach
to their thought is to consider the legal status they attributed to
poor persons, the legal consequences implied by a state of poverty
as such. Their attitude was inevitably influenced by the Church's
teaching that voluntary poverty was a form of asceticism good in
itself, a state pleasing to God. But there has sometimes been a
tendency to exaggerate the effects of this teaching on medieval
attitudes to poverty in general. Medieval men were quite capable
of distinguishing between holy poverty and idle parasitism. St.
Francis of Assisi is always cited as the extreme example of
romantic devotion to poverty almost as an end in itself, but
Francis wrote in his last testament: "I have worked with my hands
and I choose to work, and I firmly wish that all my brothers
should work at some honorable trade. And if they do not know
how, let them learn. . . ."⁹ Again, medieval men were quite
capable of distinguishing between holy voluntary poverty and
squalid involuntary want, and were well aware that the latter
state was not likely to be productive of the higher moral virtues.
The theologians were in the habit of pointing out that a state of
involuntary poverty gave rise to strong temptations to theft and
perjury. Among the canonists, Huguccio, who wrote the greatest
of the twelfth-century commentaries on the *Decretum* (*ca.* 1188),
divided the poor into three categories. Some were born poor but
willingly endured their poverty for the love of God. Others joined
themselves to the poor by giving up all their possessions to follow
Christ. These two kinds of poverty were called voluntary. But
there was a third sort of poor who were filled only with "the
voracity of cupidity." That sort of poverty was called necessary
or involuntary.¹⁰ It was well understood that the experience of
poverty, like the experience of pain, might bring spiritual enrichment to a man who was capable of accepting it voluntarily, but
also that, in itself, poverty was an unpleasant affliction which might
produce quite opposite effects.

While, however, idleness was condemned and poverty was not
automatically equated with virtue, there was no disposition to go

to the opposite extreme and assume that a state of destitution was necessarily indicative of moral turpitude. It hardly ever occurred to the canonists that the law should seek to "deter" men from falling into poverty. Want was its own deterrent, they thought. And it never occurred to them at all that poverty was a vice which could be stamped out by punitive measures. They no more thought of punishing a man for being afflicted with poverty than we would think of punishing a man for being afflicted with tuberculosis. There is obviously a sharp divergence here between the basic presuppositions of medieval law and those of the poor law in more recent times. As late as 1909 the authors of the majority report of an English royal commission proceeded on the assumption that every instance of destitution implied "a defect in the citizen character." In such a climate of thought it was natural that the status of pauperism came to imply not only a social stigma, but also definite legal disabilities. The pauper became a sort of second-class citizen.[11] The canonists, on the other hand, proceeded implicitly on the opposite assumption in all their discussions of the status of a poor man before the law courts, and sometimes were led to formulate explicitly a very different doctrine. Joannes Andreae, author of the *Glossa Ordinaria* to the *Liber Sextus,* used a phrase that has almost the ring of a challenge thrown down in advance to all the subsequent centuries of punitive and deterrent poor law: "Poverty is not a kind of crime." [12]

This principle was derived from a text of St. Ambrose, included in the *Decretum,* which dealt with the factors involving an individual in criminal guilt. St. Ambrose argued that moral evil could only be imputed when there was evil intent of the mind. "Only those things are evil that involve the mind in crime." [13] Accordingly, such things as poverty, low birth, and sickness were not numbered among the things evil in this sense. In another part of the *Decretum,* however, Gratian cited a text of Roman law which included the poor among the classes of persons who were considered unworthy to present an accusation before a court of law. Gratian let this pass without comment, but Joannes Teutonicus, discussing this passage in his *Glossa Ordinaria* (*ca.* 1216), held that a poor man could be barred from acting as accuser only if his integrity was suspect; poverty itself was not a sufficient reason for excluding him. The same was true, according to Joannes, when it was a question of receiving the testimony of a poor man as a witness. To support these views he cited the opinion of St. Ambrose and, adapting the saint's own words, maintained, "Paupertas non est de numero malorum," "Poverty is not among the number of things evil," that is, things criminal or morally reprehensible.[14] A century later Joannes Andreae modified the phrase a little further to the words already cited, "Poverty is not a kind of crime" ("Paupertas non est de genere malorum").

It followed naturally from this principle that the law relating to the status of poor persons should have as its main object the maintenance of their legal rights. Then, as now, the very fact of being poor put a man at a disadvantage when he sought redress of wrong or was compelled to defend himself before a court of law. The canonists sought to minimize the disadvantage as far as possible. Poor persons were exempted from paying the substantial court fees that normally made medieval justice, like modern justice, an expensive commodity. Pope Honorius III (1216–1227) laid down further that litigants too poor to provide themselves with legal counsel were to be supplied with free counsel by the court.[15] Priests were normally forbidden to plead before the law courts, but a special exception was made when they undertook to defend a poor man's case, and, similarly, as an exception to the general rule, a priest was allowed to conduct his own case before the courts if he was too poor to hire an agent to act on his behalf.[16]

Although a poor man could not be rejected as a witness simply because of his poverty, Pope Eugenius III (1145–1153) decreed that the judges were not to compel him to appear in court. The decretal ran like this: "If any of the witnesses are old and infirm or weakened by sickness or oppressed by poverty so that they cannot be brought before you, you are to send worthy and discreet persons to receive [their testimony]."[17] Presumably the pope simply meant that when a poor man would be put to some hardship by wasting a day in court he was to be excused, but the canonists found this a difficult text to interpret, for, after all, a poor witness could be compensated for lost time. Bernardus

Parmensis, author of the *Glossa Ordinaria* to the Decretals of
Gregory IX, raised the question why the poor should be thus
excused. "Even though they are poor, they can well come," he
wrote. His solution is revealing. There were some for whom it
was not fitting that they should come to court because they were
gentle folk (*nobilis*) and so were ashamed to come in great
poverty; but, he hastened to add, such a poor man was really an
honorable person, and was not to be held suspect solely on account
of his poverty.[18] This illustrates a common attitude of the canonists.
They knew that a man of good estate who fell into poverty would
feel a sense of shame, but since poverty itself was not morally
reprehensible, the Church ought not to add to that shame, but
should spare him embarrassment as far as possible. Hostiensis,
one of the greatest jurists of the mid-thirteenth century, repeated
this argument of Bernardus Parmensis, and then put forward
another solution. He suggested that the words "oppressed by
poverty" in the pope's decretal might refer to the poverty of a
litigant rather than of a witness. Perhaps one of the principals
in the suit was too poor to pay the expenses of the witnesses needed
to establish his case, and that was the reason why the court was
to send messengers to receive their testimony.[19] Some of the later
canonists held that the court should pay the expenses of witnesses
needed by a poor litigant, as well as provide him with free
counsel.[20] Gradually, indeed, a whole array of technical privileges
came to be attributed to a poor man facing an ecclesiastical court.
A substantial list was given by Guido de Baysio in his *Rosarium*.[21]

The canonists not only sought to protect the interests of a poor
litigant in a church court; they were also concerned to ensure that,
whenever a man was likely to suffer injustice on account of his
poverty, his case should be decided before a church court rather
than before a secular one. I have already emphasized the tendency
of church courts to extend their own jurisdiction. The secular
authorities naturally resisted what they regarded as encroachments,
and, indeed, the whole vast problem of Church and state, a problem
that is still very much with us, tended to present itself in the
Middle Ages as a problem of competing jurisdictions. The canonists' claim that church courts should redress the wrongs of all

poor persons, even lay folk, is a minor and little explored byway of the whole controversy, but it has perhaps more significance than its intrinsic importance would at first sight suggest. The canonists, on the whole, have not received very sympathetic treatment from historians. On the high level of papal policy it can be argued that their claims tended merely to entangle the Papacy in a struggle for worldly power which could only compromise its true spiritual mission. On the lower level of petty litigation, it is obvious that any extension of ecclesiastical jurisdiction meant more business for the canon lawyers themselves, so that their claims could have arisen from the crudest sort of self-interest. But there was no political advantage to be gained by extending the protection of church courts to poor lay folk. Poor men had no votes in those days. Nor was there any financial advantage. Poor men paid no fees. When, therefore, we read the complex canonistic arguments about justice for the poor, we may be persuaded that the canonists, in spite of the worldly and self-seeking motives that no doubt did exist, were as a class motivated at bottom by a conviction that their own system of law best exemplified the rules of equity and justice, and that the order and harmony of Christendom could best be maintained by maximizing the influence of church courts. It was not an ignoble end that they pursued, even though some of their particular claims may strike oddly on the modern ear.

There was general agreement among the canonists that the Church had a special duty to protect the class of people they called *miserabiles personae*, "wretched persons"—"poor wretches," we might say. The term was used of widows and orphans in particular, and of all the poor and oppressed in general. As Gratian himself put it, "The bishop ought to be solicitous and vigilant concerning the defense of the poor and the relief of the oppressed." [22] The technical problem was to define how far the Church could claim a right of interference in the normal processes of secular jurisdiction in order to attain this end.

In the broader problems of Church and state, the canonists tended to move from ambiguous and moderate positions in the twelfth century to more explicit and more extreme ones in the thirteenth, and it was the same in this matter. The position was at first very confused. Joannes Teutonicus, author of the *Glossa Ordinaria* to the *Decretum*, was a subtle and resourceful canonist, but if the various texts of his gloss touching on this question are brought together they give the impression that for once he was downright baffled. The difficulty was not only that, in actual practice, secular courts naturally claimed jurisdiction over the temporal affairs of laymen whether they were poor or not, but also that some of the early texts incorporated in the *Decretum* referred to kings and emperors as well as to bishops and popes as the natural protectors of the poor. The canon of the *Decretum* which most clearly set out the duty of the Church to offer legal redress to the poor was taken from the ninth-century council of Toulouse, and it ran like this: "If any powerful man shall have despoiled a cleric, or a poor man, or a monk, and the bishop has commanded him to come to judgment and he has disdained to do so, . . . he shall be held excommunicate until he obeys and makes restitution." Joannes Teutonicus commented on this a little dubiously: "It seems therefore that cases of oppression of poor men belong to the Church," and he added a reference to *Distinctio* 87 of the *Decretum*. At this point he observed: "Note that cases of the poor and oppressed and of pilgrims belong to the Church. . . . They also belong to the judgment of the king," and gave a string of references to justify both assertions. This was not very helpful. Joannes' next suggestion was that cases of poor men could be brought before a church court only after an attempt had been made to obtain justice before a secular one. But this raised another difficulty. According to the canonists anyone at all could appeal to a church court if the secular authorities refused to do justice in his case. It seemed, therefore, that the *miserabiles personae* enjoyed no particular advantage from the fact that they were said to be under ecclesiastical protection. Joannes posed this objection but found himself unable to answer it. At still another point he wrote that cases of the poor belonged to both jurisdictions, "but more to the Church." In fact, he did not succeed in making up his mind or in reconciling the divergent texts.[23]

It seems worth while to pursue this tangled argument in some little detail, both because it is interesting in itself and because it provides a good preliminary example of canonistic method. Here is an instance where the texts of the *Decretum* provide no clear-cut solution of a serious problem; the glossator tries to find a solution by bringing together the various texts that can be cited on both sides of the argument, but he has no real success. When this situation arises one will usually find new papal rulings on the point at issue assembled in the Decretals of Gregory IX to provide a basis for further discussion, and an eventual solution arrived at through the drawing of subtler distinctions and subdistinctions.

There were in fact several texts of the Decretals bearing on the problem, and two of special importance. The first dealt with a certain Lady Juliana. Juliana became involved in a suit against another lady over disputed property rights and succeeded in having the case brought before a church court on the plea that she was a poor widow. The opposing party pointed out, however, that although Juliana was a widow she was by no means poor. She was in fact noble and rich and, it was implied, quite capable of looking after herself without any special protection from the Church. The ecclesiastical judges therefore refused to hear the case.[24] The second case also dealt with a distinguished lady, Berengaria, widow of King Richard the Lion Heart of England. She claimed that a neighboring count had seized one of her castles in France, and she appealed to the pope to compel him to make restitution. The count objected that the widow had no right to invoke the power of the Church in such a case unless the appropriate feudal lord had been appealed to and had refused to do justice. The pope, however, did not accept this argument. When a widow's property had been seized by violence the Church would immediately take action to compel restitution. Medieval law distinguished sharply between a possessory action which determined only the immediate right of occupation of disputed property, and the subsequent litigation which would establish ultimate rights of ownership. Pope Honorius had this distinction in mind; he thought the intervention of the Church justified in this case because only a possessory action was involved. In other circumstances the count's objection would have been valid.[25]

These two decretals provided important new arguments. The

first raised the question whether ecclesiastical intervention was to be based on a technical status like widowhood, or on a condition of real poverty and need. The second decretal indicated that the accessibility of church courts to *miserabiles personae* would depend on the type of action involved. Together they provided a much more adequate basis for defining the technical implications of the "protection" that the Church was supposed to extend to "wretched persons." The comments of Bernardus Parmensis in his *Glossa Ordinaria* were not very enterprising,[26] but Pope Innocent IV, who wrote an influential commentary on the Decretals about 1250, was much more penetrating in his analysis. All this discussion of noble ladies and royal widows seems to have drifted far from the problems and the legal status of the ordinary humble poor. Innocent brought them back again to the center of the discussion. In considering the case of Lady Juliana, he insisted on a distinction between the really poor and those who, although laboring under some handicap, were financially well-to-do; he mentioned among others widows and orphans, the old, the blind, the mutilated, and those worn down by long sickness. These were technically *miserabiles personae* but they were not necessarily poor and powerless. Innocent maintained that the really poor, those in genuine need, should be allowed to bring their cases before church courts as a general rule, and not only when it was a question of obtaining restitution of something seized by violence. But persons who were rich, although technically *miserabiles personae*, could normally appeal to the Church only after they had attempted to obtain justice from the appropriate secular court and had failed to gain satisfaction through the malice or negligence of the judge.

Innocent also answered the question raised by Joannes Teutonicus: What advantage did these "wretched persons" have compared with other litigants? He explained that a litigant could normally appeal to the church courts only in the last resort; if a secular judge refused to do justice in his case he was required to appeal to a superior judge, and then, if necessary, appeal again until every resource of secular justice had been exhausted. But the Church would deal with the case of any *miserabilis persona* after the first failure to obtain justice. Again, Innocent observed that he would not have the church courts hear the case even of a genuinely poor man without prior recourse to the secular authorities if the litigant, although poor in his actual possessions, was suing for some vast heritage or estate. It was the ordinary poor folk, enmeshed in their petty burdens and difficulties, whom he wanted to have free access to the church courts.[27] And so, after a century of legislation and canonistic argumentation, the vague assertions of the *Decretum* on behalf of "wretched persons" received a precise and technical legal interpretation. It is interesting that it was Innocent IV who drew the distinctions necessary to protect the really needy, for he is often presented as the very personification of the less edifying type of medieval pontiff— hard, worldly, and legalistic.

Another quite different sphere in which the canonists concerned themselves about the status of the "underprivileged" was the provision of education for the poor. Here again there is a great difference between the medieval attitude and the later trends of thought which reached their climax in the nineteenth century. In 1847 the Poor Law Commissioners in England explicitly forbade that public money should be used for the education of poor children.[28] They were afraid, apparently, that such extravagance would tend to make life altogether too soft and easy for the destitute. By way of contrast, here is a canon promulgated by Pope Alexander III in the Third Lateran Council of 1179: "Since the Church of God, like a devoted mother, is bound to provide lest the poor who cannot be helped by the labors of their parents should lose the opportunity of studying and profiting thereby, a suitable benefice is to be provided in each cathedral church for a master who shall give free instruction to the clerics of the church and to poor scholars." [29] This decree was confirmed and extended by Pope Innocent III in the Fourth Lateran Council of 1215. Innocent laid down that not only cathedral churches but all others with sufficient resources were to provide for a master who would give free instruction to poor scholars. Apart from reading and writing, these church schools would teach mainly Latin and elementary logic, the foundations of medieval education, but Innocent also required that in each metropolitan church there should be established a master competent to teach the higher science of theology.[30] The schools attached to the greater cathedrals often became the nuclei of the universities that grew up in the thirteenth century, some of which are still flourishing today among the great universities of the world.

It is true of course that medieval men did not know all the advantages—and abuses—of modern mass education. The medieval system erred by failing to educate up to the limits of their capacities the duller, less alert, and less ambitious clerics, the type that served as village priests in obscure rural parishes. But a poor boy of real intellectual ability could get an education in the Middle Ages with perhaps no more difficulties and hardships than many a modern boy overcomes in working his way through college. And if he did succeed in becoming a Master of Arts, or perhaps even a Doctor of Canon Law, there were attractive careers open to him. He might rise high in the administrative service of the king, and, above all, the Church offered unlimited opportunities of promotion to men of sufficient ability. Many of the greatest medieval churchmen, bishops, cardinals, even popes, were men of humble origin. It did help of course to be born the son of a great noble or the nephew of a cardinal, just as it helps nowadays to be born the son of a millionaire, but, because of the educational facilities that the Church provided, the channels of promotion were open to poor boys as well.

The only difficulty the canonists found in interpreting these decrees on education lay in defining the precise extent of a professor's obligation to teach without exacting any fees. He certainly had to teach the poor without charge, but what about the rich? The argument was put forward that knowledge was a gift of God; therefore, to sell it for money was sinful, a sort of simony. And since most of these canonistic writers were professors themselves the point was obviously a delicate one. Joannes Teutonicus, in his gloss on the *Decretum*, suggested that a teacher could take fees only if he was actually in want, but Bartholomaeus Brixiensis, who wrote additional notes on the *Glossa Ordinaria*, would have none of this and held that a teacher was always entitled to payment from those who could afford it.[31] Joannes himself returned to the discussion in a gloss on the canon of the Fourth Lateran Council, and this time he provided a detailed analysis which was generally accepted. When a teacher was provided with an adequate income by a church he was strictly bound to teach without fees only to the clerics of the church and to poor scholars. It was for their sakes that his income was provided, not for the sakes of the rich. But, in these circumstances, it would be more honorable and praiseworthy for the master to offer his services freely to all. If, on the other hand, a scholar was teaching as a private master without an income from the church it was entirely proper for him to take fees from his pupils. He received payment, not for "selling knowledge," but as a reasonable compensation for the time and labor expended. In the same way a judge received payment for carrying out the duties of his office, but he was not said to sell justice.[32] Joannes' final conclusion was, in effect, that the laborer is worthy of his hire—even a professor.

It was suggested at the outset that the study of medieval law could serve as an introduction to a world of ideas far removed from our own. Yet in discussing topics like legal aid, educational opportunities, and professors' salaries we seem to be concerned with problems that are thoroughly contemporary. And when we bear in mind the principle that underlay the canonists' treatment of such themes—"Poverty is not a kind of crime"—it may seem that their approach to social problems was closer to ours than that of our own great-grandfathers. This is only a half-truth. The world of the Middle Ages is so remote from our own that it does indeed require a real effort of the imagination to understand medieval patterns of life and thought; yet it is not so alien as to be altogether irrelevant. That is the special fascination of medieval studies. Medieval men are our ancestors in the spirit as well as in the flesh. These apparently dead thoughts which we laboriously resuscitate have exerted a lasting influence on the living tradition of Christian civilization we have inherited. By studying that tradition we can come to understand some of the factors that have helped to make the modern world in the very act of learning to stand outside it.

CHAPTER

11 *Property*

It seems to be the fashion in modern works on social welfare to emphasize that problems of poverty can be successfully attacked only when they are considered, not independently, but as integral factors in "the total social process," which is no doubt true enough. It seems more than a fashion—almost a tradition—to observe that ecclesiastical theories of poor relief have generally neglected the broader social aspects of the subject. Twenty-five years ago a distinguished Protestant theologian, in a course of lectures on the contribution of religion to social work, complained that in the medieval Church "there was no thought of the reorganization of society in the interest of a greater justice." [1] More recently, a distinguished Catholic historian has felt it necessary to explain that the medieval Church was not an institution dedicated primarily to the cause of social reform and that "the church, therefore, did not condemn feudalism and serfdom." [2] The implication seems to be that if the Church had been really alert to major social problems, it would naturally have condemned feudalism out of hand, and, presumably, would have agitated for equality, democracy, individual free enterprise, and an industrial revolution.

The truth is that medieval theologians and canonists were exceptionally far-ranging in their treatment of social and economic questions. A modern textbook on sociology will pose few fundamental problems that did not arise in one form or another in the theological *Summa* of St. Thomas Aquinas or in the canonistic *Commentaria* of Hostiensis. The real reason that such gifted thinkers did not condemn the whole established organization of society is the rather obvious one that, on the whole, in that particular historical and economic context, the existing hierarchical

structure was the best adapted to promote the general welfare
and to sustain the complex and brilliant culture of the high Middle
Ages. The medieval peasant was usually very poor, but that was
more a result of the primitive state of agricultural technology than
of a defective organization of society. He sometimes suffered
from the violence of warring lords, but violence was endemic in
a society only a few generations removed from the raw barbarism
of the Dark Ages. The problem was to mitigate it so as to permit
as much decent and orderly life as possible, and a system of feudal
obligations, backed by an effective royal administration such as
existed in France and England in the thirteenth century, provided
the best available solution. The notions of modern American
democracy, if they could have occurred to anyone, would naturally
have been dismissed as mischievous irrelevancies, just as the feudal
apparatus of homage and vassalage would seem irrelevant in modern industrial America.

The canonistic doctrine on poor relief, considered for the moment
simply as a theoretical structure of ideas, is especially interesting
precisely because it was firmly rooted in a broader philosophy
of property and society. In every age the prevailing assumptions
concerning the proper distribution, control, and social obligations
of property naturally influence the measures adopted for the relief
of poverty. And, conversely, every theory of poor relief implies
a theory of property. One can find a good illustration of this in a
paper by Mary Richmond, well known to social workers as a
pioneer in the Charity Organization Movement—though the theory
of property implied would probably not have been altogether approved by Miss Richmond herself. The year 1893 was one of
great unemployment in New York; some of the newspapers organized and advertised relief funds, and made their offices centers
for the distribution of food and clothing to the poor. Mary Richmond referred to this experience in a memorandum prepared for
the 1921 White House conference on unemployment. In the memorandum she quoted the criticisms made by experienced social
workers of the newspapers' efforts at the time. The criticisms were
partly directed against administrative inefficiencies, but the fundamental one was that the newspapers' relief arrangements encour-

aged the poor to think that they had a *right* to food and clothes, that such gifts were not "favors received" from the rich, but something due, something owed.[3]

The philosophy of property implied in this criticism is perfectly clear-cut. If one man has ten million dollars and another man is starving in the streets outside his house, the first man has an absolute legal right to every one of his dollars and the second man has no right whatsoever to any of them. If the first man chooses to give the other a dollar, the poor man should be properly grateful as for a "favor received." In its way the doctrine is impartial and balanced, however, for it holds that the starving man also has an equal and absolute right to own ten million dollars, if he can find any legal way to acquire them.

Often, of course, the philosophy of property implied in a given approach to problems of poor relief remains merely implicit. But in the canonists' writings it was explicitly stated and intricately worked out to form a philosophical foundation for their ideas on the relief of poverty. It is this kind of intellectual underpinning, this legal philosophy of property, that we must consider before we turn to the more concrete problems of medieval poor law.

It may be helpful to discuss first some aspects of property ownership as it existed in actual practice in the Middle Ages. The system was different from both modern individual proprietorship and modern socialist collectivism. Medieval men certainly recognized individual rights in property, but the holding of property usually involved the owner in a complex of social and economic obligations. On the lowest level the medieval peasant, the serf or villein, held strips of arable land from the lord of the manor— perhaps 20 or 30 acres. He also had a right to pasture his beasts on the common land of the village, and a right to share in the produce of the village hayfield. In return he owed various services to the lord of the manor, especially the duty of working on the lord's land for a fixed number of days in the week. The precise services due were determined by the custom of the manor, and disputes were dealt with in the manor court. The great disadvantage in the serf's position was that he was not free to leave the manor on which he was born. He was "bound to the soil," as the medieval phrase went. It must have been an irksome restriction to the more ambitious spirits, but there were two safety valves. Any serf who fled to a town and lived there for a year and a day became a free man. His lord had no further claim on him. And a serf who became a priest also acquired free status. That required the consent of the lord, but it seems to have been not infrequently granted; certainly there were priests of servile origin in the Middle Ages. Looking at the situation from the standpoint of the twentieth century we are prone to emphasize the limitation on the individual freedom of the ordinary serf in that he was bound to the soil. For many medieval peasants it must have seemed far more important that the soil was bound to the serf. They did resent forced-labor services and sought to commute them for money rents while retaining permanency of tenure, but a mere abstract liberty to wander away and perhaps starve on the roads would not have seemed nearly so attractive to the average peasant as the solid right that he actually enjoyed to farm his own small holding and, in due time, to pass it on to his heirs.

The medieval peasant's standard of life must often have been close to a bare subsistence level, and in years of bad harvest he would know real hunger, but his rights in his own land did provide a certain minimum of security and stability. It is important to bear in mind something of this background not only to understand medieval theories of property, but also to appreciate the kind of poverty that would commonly occur in medieval society and so to judge the effectiveness of the measures proposed for its relief.[4] It must be remembered too that, although commerce was flourishing in the thirteenth century compared with previous centuries, and towns were growing in importance, the vast majority of medieval men still lived in small self-contained and almost self-supporting agricultural communities.

There were analogous relationships higher up on the social scale. The relationship of the peasant to the lord of the manor was servile, whereas that of the lord of the manor to his feudal lord was honorable, a relationship between gentlemen who were expected to hold one another in mutual respect. Yet there were certain similarities. The lord of the manor held his estate from a superior lord, a baron or perhaps the king himself, to whom he in turn owed specified services. In the classical feudal pattern the service owed was military; the knight rode to battle in the service of his lord in return for the lands he held. By the thirteenth century a money payment was often substituted for personal military service, but still the relationship was not merely an economic one. The knight was bound by a solemn oath of loyalty to his lord, and was involved in a whole network of social and legal obligations arising from his tenure.

A final important point in connection with property ownership in the high Middle Ages is that, through the accumulated endowments of centuries, the Church had become one of the greatest of proprietors. Cathedral churches and monasteries in particular sometimes owned land on a scale that made the bishop or abbot equal in economic resources, as well as in social prestige, to a great feudal baron. This situation, although usually accepted as normal and proper, did evoke criticism in some quarters, especially among the more extreme sections of the Franciscan order. These extremists emphasized the virtue of poverty in the religious life in such a fashion as to imply a condemnation of the established Church with its worldly wealth and organized government. The canonists, for their part, generally accepted the existing structure of property relationships as necessary and just. They were therefore concerned to defend a system in which individual rights in property were clearly acknowledged, but with corresponding obligations, and in which the Church was a very substantial property holder.

The principal difficulty that they encountered in this task did not lie in meeting the criticisms of contemporary radicals, but in framing an acceptable doctrine of property which would be consistent with the old texts of the *Decretum* itself. Some of the writings of the church Fathers which Gratian cited were so violent in protesting against the abuses of wealth that they seemed to imply a condemnation of all private property; and in the *Decretum* there were also references to the primitive communism of the early Christians as described in the Acts of the Apostles.[5] For instance, a letter supposedly written by the first-century St. Clement to the Christians of Jerusalem runs like this:

The common life, brethren, is necessary for all and especially for those who desire to serve God blamelessly and who wish to imitate the life of the Apostles and their disciples. The use of all things that are in the world ought to be common to all men. But through sin one man claimed this as his own and another that, and so division was made among men. Again, a certain very wise Greek, knowing these things to be, said all things ought to be common among friends. . . . And just as the air cannot be divided, he said, nor the splendor of the sun, so the other things of the world which were given to be held in common by all ought not to be divided.

After this reminiscence of Plato, the letter goes on to describe the life of the first Christians in the days of the Apostles:

There was no one among us in need. But all who owned houses or fields sold them and brought the proceeds with anything else they had and laid them at the feet of the Apostles . . . and they were divided among individuals according to their need. . . . Wherefore we command you to take note of these things, and to obey the doctrines and examples of the Apostles.[6]

This was no doubt a drastically effective solution for the problem of poverty, but it was of course utterly incompatible with the actual pattern of medieval economic life. The canonists were not too acutely embarrassed by the reminder of communal ownership in the early Church, nor even by the apparent fact that one of the first popes had commanded the Christians of his day to abandon private property. They were not totally devoid of historical sense and were quite capable of pointing out that economic arrangements that had been admirable and appropriate eleven or twelve centuries earlier were impracticable in the circumstances of their own age. Joannes Teutonicus, commenting on this passage, first suggested that the pope's command might be interpreted merely as advice. Then he went on: "It seems nevertheless that this was a command because the primitive Church could command this, like continence; but if this were commanded nowadays it would cripple the state of the universal Church, which ought not to be." [7]

It was not so much the historical precedent set out in this letter as the philosophic implications of the argument which entangled the canonists in difficulties. They were very much concerned about the suggestion that private property was somehow contrary to the divine will. It seemed plausible to argue that, from the very beginning, God had created the earth for all men —not only for this man or for that man—and had intended them all to share in its fruits, just as God's sunshine is common to all, and the air that we breathe. Such an argument implied that no man ought to be excluded from any part of the earth by the property rights of another. It was not so much primitive communism as a kind of philosophic anarchism that the canonists had to explain and, if possible, explain away. In their own language the essential problem was that private property, according to some texts, seemed contrary to the law of nature. The importance in the present context of their complex and rather rarefied arguments on the problem of the rights and obligations inherent in property ownership is that it was precisely in discussing the abstract theory of property that the canonists developed the conceptions that were to shape their practical doctrine of charity.

The idea of natural law was familiar to all medieval thinkers. It was capable of the most subtle ramifications and diverse interpretations, but there was always present the fundamental belief that, in the beginning, God had implanted in the very nature of things, and especially in the nature of man, norms of conduct that were more binding than any mere human laws. The whole problem of natural law and its relation to private property was raised in the opening pages of the *Decretum*. Gratian's very first words were these:

The human race is ruled by two [principles], namely by natural law and by customs. Natural law is that which is contained in the Law and the Gospels, by which each one is commanded to do to others what he wishes to be done to himself, and is forbidden to do to others what he does not wish done to himself. [8]

He then cited a series of texts from St. Isidore of Seville defining natural law and the different varieties of human law. The definition of natural law went like this:

Natural law is common to all nations, so that it is held everywhere by instinct of nature, not by any legal enactment—as, for instance, the coming together of men and women, the succession and rearing of children, *the common possession of all things*, the one liberty of all, the acquisition of whatever is taken by air, land, or sea, the restitution of goods or money loaned, the repelling of force by force.[9]

The "common possession of all things" is here described as a part of "natural law," but it is obvious that the term "natural law" is being used in a wide variety of senses, some of which have nothing to do with Gratian's own original definition. Apparently unaware of these complexities, Gratian serenely forged ahead with his argument. After describing many varieties of human law, he continued: "Natural law holds primacy over all others in time and in dignity, for it commenced from the beginning of rational creatures, nor does it vary with time, but remains immutable." [10] Gratian's own thought seems to have been that natural law consisted of the fundamental moral principles implied by the text, "Do unto others as you would have them do unto you," principles which were laid down for Christians in the Bible, but which were inherent in the rational nature of man and so common to all peoples.

When he came to deal explicitly with the relationship of natural law to private property, Gratian wrote: "Natural law differs from customs and enactments, for by natural law all things are common to all men. . . . By the laws of custom and legal enactment, this belongs to me, that to another." In proof of this assertion Gratian next quoted a text of St. Augustine:

By divine law, "The Lord's is the earth and the fullness thereof." Poor and rich God made from one dust, and poor and rich the one earth supports. Nevertheless by human law we say, "This farm is mine, this house is mine, this slave is mine." Now human laws are the laws of the emperors. Why? Because God distributes these human laws to the human race through the emperors and kings of the world.[11]

He at once added to this another comment of his own: "Likewise in dignity natural law is superior to custom or legal enactment. For whatever things are received as custom or included in written law, if they are contrary to natural law, they are to be held null and void." Gratian seems to have led us into a sort of logical ambush. By natural law all property is common, and private rights rest on human law. But human law contrary to natural law is to be held null and void. The conclusion seems inescapable that private property rights are null and void. Evidently no formal poor law needed to be or could be elaborated if every man had a simple right to help himself to whatever he wanted.

Gratian had left quite a tangle for the decretists to unravel. He was not really preaching communism, or anarchism, to the prosperous prelates and nobles of his own age. In other parts of the *Decretum* he took it for granted that property rights were valid and were properly protected by law. As the commentators were fond of pointing out, the Bible itself provided plenty of evidence that private property was licit. A command like "Thou shalt not covet thy neighbor's goods" implied clearly enough that the neighbor had rights in his own property which had to be respected. Even the text of St. Augustine, which Gratian cited to prove that the institution of private property rested on merely human law, reveals quite clearly that St. Augustine did not regard this human law as contrary to the divine scheme of things, for he regarded the kings and emperors who promulgated it as agents of the divine will.

The crux of the problem is this. Gratian himself began by using the term "natural law" to describe the immutable moral principles proper to rational creatures, but the texts he cited, in which community of property was described as a rule of natural law, were using the term in a quite different sense. Later on in the twelfth century it became almost an academic game among canonists to find as many different meanings as possible for the expression "natural law," [12] but there are two fundamental ones whose confusion has ensnared thinkers more recent and more renowned perhaps than the author of the *Decretum*. The word "natural" can be used to describe the original, the primitive condition of man, untouched by the sophisticated conventions of civilization; or it can be used to describe the qualities appropriate in a creature of man's peculiar nature, his intellectual and spiritual nature, that is. The one usage refers to the origin of man, the other to the destiny of man. Only the concept of natural law in the second sense can have any claim to provide an immutable moral code. The first definition is merely descriptive of a supposed early state of society.[13] By failing to distinguish clearly between what he considered primitive in human society and what he considered proper for human society, Gratian enmeshed himself in much the same semantic muddle as some of the eighteenth-century *philosophes*. One half expects to find a Noble Savage peeping out from the tangled undergrowth of decretist texts.

The canonists' own brand of semantic analysis, the minute definition of all the possible meanings of a given term with appropriate distinctions and subdistinctions, made for a tedious literary style, but it was very well adapted to cope with this particular problem. Indeed, although Gratian himself never explicitly dealt with the issue raised by his texts, there was a solution implicit in his words, "Natural law holds primacy *in time* and in dignity." The *Summa Parisiensis*, written probably in 1159, expanded this point. According to the author of this work, when community of property is said to be prescribed by divine law, "divine law is here to be interpreted strictly, namely as the natural law that existed in the beginning, that is to say, the primeval institution of things." [14] Rufinus, writing about the same time, explained that some parts of natural law consisted of commands or prohibitions, and these were indeed immutable; but other parts consisted of mere descriptions—*demonstrationes*—and there was nothing morally binding in them. In this latter category he included the natural law relating to community of property.[15] It was merely a description of a former state of society, not a command for all time. These arguments were repeated by other canonists and by theologians with various modifications and additions, and it was along these lines that in the thirteenth century St. Thomas Aquinas, whose work has usually been regarded as the classical exposition of medieval thought on natural law, formulated his solution of the problem of property. It might be argued that the abandonment of primitive communism had been made necessary by human sin, or simply that division among private owners was the most effective way of implementing the divine will that everyone should have a share in the fruits of the earth. In either event, the objection that private property was contrary to natural law could easily be circumvented by explaining that the natural law involved was merely descriptive of a primitive state of things, without permanent validity.[16]

This line of argument was quite adequate to extricate the canonists from the merely verbal inconsistencies of the *Decretum*. But, in a deeper sense, it had the disadvantage that in itself it established no relationship between natural law and the social obligations of property. It is especially interesting, therefore, that the two most influential of all the decretists, Huguccio and Joannes Teutonicus, put forward a quite different solution. This new argument was propounded by Huguccio as an alternative to the ones already considered; [17] it was accepted by Joannes Teutonicus in preference to them, and was transmitted in his *Glossa Ordinaria* to many subsequent generations of students of the *Decretum*. Before Huguccio the canonists had explained the statement, "According to natural law all things are common," by a critical analysis of the word "natural." Huguccio suggested that it might be helpful to consider in a little detail the word "common" as well. In the form of the argument presented by Joannes Teutonicus it was maintained that community of property actually was prescribed by natural law understood as a divine command or a rule of rational equity, but only in a special sense of the word "common":

To understand these things, note that "nature" is used in many senses. Sometimes "nature" refers to the power inherent in things by which like procreates like. In a second sense "nature" means the stimulus or instinct of nature proceeding from sensuality. . . . In a third sense it means the instinct of nature proceeding from reason, and the law proceeding from this "nature" is called rational equity, and according to this law of nature all things are called common, *that is they are to be shared in time of necessity* as in *Dist.*47 c.8. In a fourth sense natural

law means natural precepts like, "Thou shalt not steal," . . . and all
divine law is called natural law; and according to this law likewise all
things are called common, that is to be shared [*communia, id est communicanda*].[18]

This interpretation clearly established a connection between
the natural law theory and the obligation of charity. It would
have been unlike a medieval canonist, though, to have asserted
that property rights were limited in this way without some
respected authority to support his statement. In another gloss a
few lines further on Joannes repeated his argument that "common"
meant "to be shared in time of need," and there he claimed to find
his authority in the old Roman law. "According to the Rhodian
law," he wrote, "foodstuffs especially were common in time of
peril," and he gave a reference to the Digest of Justinian.[19] Now
this was a piece of pure legal fiction. The text of the Digest to
which he referred had nothing to do with natural law or the
rights of property in the abstract. It dealt in fact with a highly
technical point of maritime law, declaring that, when several
merchants were transporting goods in a ship, and part of the
cargo had to be thrown overboard to avoid shipwreck, all the
merchants should share the cost of the jettisoned goods. The law
explained that each merchant should be assessed in proportion to
the value of his merchandise, but not including his provisions for
use on the voyage, for, it concluded, if such things should be
lacking during the voyage, each would contribute what he possessed
to the common store. Joannes extracted these last words from their
technical context, inflated them into a general principle of equity,
and based a whole theory of natural law on them. It is a very
legalistic and artificial way of arguing, but that is the way lawyers'
minds sometimes work. Many currently enforceable rules of
English or American law are derived ultimately from such
straining of old texts. And, however clumsy the argument, it does
lead to the very important conclusion that the community of
property prescribed in natural law consists in an obligation on
property holders to share their wealth with those in need. In the
thought of Joannes Teutonicus the abstract theory of property and
the practical doctrine of charity are like the intersecting arches

that sustain a Gothic vault, with this principle as the common keystone that holds the whole structure together.

The keystone was deftly inserted in place at the text cited by Joannes in his first discussion on the point.[20] This text, attributed to St. Ambrose in the *Decretum*, brought together the two essential elements of the problem, the right to own property and the right use of property. It rebuked a rich man for saying he could do what he liked with his own wealth, cast serious doubts on his right to own property at all, and strongly emphasized his duty to help the poor:

But you say, "Where is the injustice if I diligently look after my own property without interfering with other people's?" O impudent words! Your own property, you say. What? From what stores did you bring it into this world? When you came into the light, when you came forth from your mother's womb, with what resources, with what reserves did you come endowed? No one may call his own what is common, of which, if man takes more than he needs, it is obtained by violence. . . . Who is more unjust, more avaricious, more greedy than a man who takes the food of the multitude not for his use but for his abundance and luxuries? . . . The bread that you hold back belongs to the needy, the clothes that you shut away belong to the naked, the money that you bury in the ground is the price of redeeming and freeing the wretched.[21]

This is robust language! Commenting on the words, "No one may call his own what is common," Joannes Teutonicus referred to a number of texts on the duty of charity and repeated his explanation that the word "common" meant "to be shared in time of need," with the same Roman law citation to support it. In this way he again avoided the implication of communal ownership as the normal pattern of economic organization, and his definition seems more relevant here, where the whole passage under discussion was concerned with the obligation of the rich to help the poor, than in contexts dealing with natural law and property rights in the abstract. The decretist text itself did not indeed deny the right to private property as such; rather it denied the right of anyone to appropriate as his own more than sufficed for his own needs. A man was not bound to deprive himself of his own necessities in order to help another in need, wrote Joannes in another context, though if he did so it would be a commendable act.²² He could even retain superfluities provided that others were not in want. But "in time of necessity" any superfluous wealth of an individual was to be regarded as common property, to be shared with those in need.

This was not an eccentricity of Joannes Teutonicus, thrown off in passing to explain an awkward text. He was rather giving a technical legal formulation to a patristic principle that became a fundamental tenet of medieval sociology, much discussed by other canonists and theologians. The main interest of those who developed the doctrine further was to explain what constituted "superfluities," and to define the circumstances in which the giving of alms was an absolute duty and those in which it was a voluntary act of merit. In the first half of the thirteenth century these questions seem to have been pursued most diligently among the theologians and especially in the school of Alexander of Hales. (This theological development has been studied recently in a number of important works by Ermenegildo Lio.²³) Just as the canonists had to cope with conflicting texts of Gratian, so the theologians were faced with an apparent contradiction in their standard "textbook," the Sentences of Peter Lombard, for the Sentences quoted two phrases of St. Augustine which implied quite different conceptions of the nature of almsgiving: in the first place, "Justice consists in helping the wretched," but then again, "Almsgiving is a work of mercy" ("Justitia est in subveniendo miseris," "Eleemosyna opus est misericordiae"). It was not clear therefore whether almsgiving was essentially an act of justice or an act of mercy. One way of reconciling the texts was to consider the subjective frame of mind of the giver. Stephen Langton suggested that the bestowing of alms on a man in need was in itself an act of bare justice, but that if the donor were actuated by a spirit of good will and fellow feeling for the recipient, then the act could at the same time be one of mercy. More commonly the theologians emphasized the same objective criterion that Joannes Teutonicus suggested. If a rich man gave to a beggar from his superfluities, it was an act of justice, for the beggar received only what was properly his own. But if a man gave away his own necessities to another, that kind of almsgiving constituted an act of mercy. It was a formulation of this commonly accepted doctrine by St. Thomas Aquinas that most influenced the writings of subsequent canonists on the question. Guido de Baysio in his *Rosarium,* a massive commentary on the *Decretum* completed in 1300, cited St. Thomas in presenting his own view that to give alms was in some circumstances a strict obligation:

The reason for this is that, since love of our neighbor is a matter of precept, everything must fall under that precept without which love of our neighbor is not preserved. But it pertains to the love of our neighbor that we should not merely wish well but act well toward him . . . and to wish well and act well toward anyone requires that we should help him in time of need. . . .

Guido concluded his argument thus: "Say briefly it is a precept to give alms from our superfluities and also to give to a man in extreme necessity. . . . To give alms in other circumstances is a matter of counsel." [24] Henricus de Bohic, in mid-fourteenth century, explained a little more carefully what was meant by superfluities: "We are bound to give what is superfluous to our own needs and the needs of our dependents, having regard to our station in life." [25] William Lyndwood, in the fifteenth century, went into more elaborate detail in his definitions. He explained that a state of extreme need existed whenever a man lacked the means of subsistence—he did not have to be actually at the point of death. Lyndwood also quoted with approval the view of St. Thomas that extreme need should be held to exist when there were evident indications that a man would be reduced to that state in the future unless help were extended. "We are not to wait for a state of ultimate necessity, because then, perhaps, it may not be possible to assist nature, worn down by hunger and thirst." As for the superfluities of the donor, Lyndwood defined these as all that was left after he had provided for his own necessities and for those of his dependents, and for all the obligations incumbent upon him. He added that a man, in computing what was necessary for himself and his family, ought not to take into account every possible future contingency, but only those things that were probable and of frequent occurrence.[26]

The canonists accepted wholeheartedly the principle that super-fluous property belonged to the poor, but they never saw in it any egalitarian implications. They never taught that there should be an average dead-level standard of living and that everyone above that standard should be stripped of his "superfluities" in order to bring him down to it. Medieval society was hierarchical in structure, and medieval canonists took it for granted that differ-ent styles of living were appropriate to the different grades in the hierarchy. At one point Joannes Teutonicus himself, commenting on an early decree that a bishop should keep only a poor household and table, observed that things were different in his own day, that bishops had ample possessions, and that the law explicitly laid down that an archbishop should travel with an escort of fifty mounted retainers.[27] Joannes Andreae made a similar point in his gloss on the *Liber Sextus*. A canon of Bologna Cathedral could live without absolute penury on twenty-five florins a year, he wrote, but he could not maintain himself becomingly on less than a hun-dred. "And," added Joannes, "I might say the same about my-self."[28]

But a man who accumulated superfluous wealth beyond what he needed to live in a decent and fitting fashion according to his status had no right to keep that wealth. He *owed* it to the poor. The *Decretum* and its *Glossa Ordinaria* bristle with phrases like this: "Feed the poor. If you do not feed them, you kill them." "Our superfluities belong to the poor." "Whatever you have beyond what suffices for your needs belongs to others." "A man who keeps for himself more than he needs is guilty of theft."[29] I think that the canonists, lacking any subtle theories about capital accumula-tion and its possible effects on productivity (which for the most part would have had little relevance in a feudal society), took these phrases in a very simple and concrete sense. They assumed that there was a given amount of food and other goods available. A man who acquired more than was due to him was therefore necessarily depriving someone else of his fair share. He was literally guilty of theft.

These arguments determined the canonists' attitude to one of the privotal problems of all poor law systems. They believed that

the poor had a *right* to be supported from the superfluous wealth
of the community. They even taught that a man in extreme need
who took the property of another was not guilty of any crime.
He was not stealing what belonged to another but only taking what
properly belonged to himself.[30] These questions were again matters
of debate among the theologians, and modern scholars who have
explored their works have insisted that, when the theologians
described almsgiving as an act of justice, they did not have in
mind any strictly juridical meaning of the word "justice" nor any
conception of "social justice." [31] They did not, that is to say, refer
to an obligation that was legally enforceable in the courts nor
oriented toward the common good, but only to a duty of an individual toward his neighbor, the fulfillment of which might in
some circumstances be a matter of strict moral obligation. However that may be, it is certain that some of the canonists were
already attempting, by the beginning of the thirteenth century,
to define the obligation of the rich toward the poor in juridical
terms. In discussing that obligation Joannes Teutonicus cited the
Roman law dictum: "It is expedient for the commonwealth
[*respublica*] that a man should not use his own property badly"; [32]
and Joannes also addressed himself to the question whether the
rich could be compelled to fulfill their duty of contributing to
the support of the poor by juridical process. This was an important point for the canonists, for, from a lawyer's point of view,
there was a major flaw in the theory that a poor man had a
right to the superfluous wealth of the rich. There did not exist any
established form of legal action by which he could sue to enforce
his right. Joannes Teutonicus therefore explained that the poor
man, though he could not obtain satisfaction "by direct judgment,"
could denounce to the Church a man who refused to give alms,
and the Church could compel him to give, presumably by ecclesiastical censures, and, in the last resort, by excommunication.[33] The
procedure of *denunciatio evangelica* here recommended by Joannes
was a form of equitable process, devised by the canonists, through
which a man could obtain redress when he was sinned against but
lacked formal grounds for an action at law.

It may be that this particular canonical remedy was more a piece of legal theory than a practical mode of ensuring adequate support for the poor in normal circumstances. But the canonists' general doctrine on the obligations of property was by no means ignored, for the Middle Ages saw a great outpouring of private charity, not only in casual almsgiving but in the endowment of permanent institutions for the care of the poor. The doctrine that the poor man had a right to the help he received was important in another way. It colored the whole relationship between benefactor and beneficiary in the Middle Ages, tending to discourage both sentimental self-esteem on the part of the donor and excessive humiliation in the recipient. That is true either of relationships in the field of private charity or of relationships within a system of public relief, for, as will be seen, the canonists did have a theory of public relief too. There is one final point to be noted about their doctrine on property. Although it professed to be based entirely on ancient authorities, a mixture of church Fathers and Roman law, it was in fact very much in harmony with the prevailing ideas on property holding exemplified in the real life of their own day. The medieval system acknowledged individual rights in property but with corresponding social obligations. The result of the canonists' analysis was to uphold the right of private property as such, but to impose one further obligation on the property owner—the duty of contributing to the support of the needy.

So far I have been dealing with the ownership of property in general. The canonists encountered problems of a different sort when they dealt with church property in particular; and here again there was a good deal of technical argumentation issuing eventually in a solution that has the greatest relevance for medieval poor law. The special difficulty concerning church property was that the canonists would never concede any right of absolute ownership to the bishop or priest who administered the revenues of a church. They insisted that he could not treat the goods of the church as his own; he could not bestow them on his family, say, or bequeath them by will, or squander them at his own pleasure. The prelate had to be defined as in some sense a trustee acting on behalf of the real owner. The main problem for the canonists was to define who actually did own the property of the Church.

It was in the twelfth century, when the sophisticated conceptions of Roman law began to influence the canonists, that the issue became prominent. In earlier times men were content to say that the owner of a church's property was the patron saint of the church; they would bequeath money to St. Peter or St. Paul when they endowed a church of that name. Or sometimes the church building was held to be a sort of embodiment of the Church as an institution, and was regarded as a legal entity capable of receiving endowments. The early comments of the church Fathers that were included in the *Decretum* provided useful indications, but they did not themselves solve the problem. The patristic works often observed that property given to the Church was given to God. No one doubted that this was true, but the canonists felt obliged to point out that everything in the world belonged to God, and even if they added, as they sometimes did, that church property belonged to God in a more special sense than any other, that was still far from a precise legal definition. Again, the early Fathers often referred to the property of the Church as "the patrimony of the poor," and this thought appeared several times in the *Decretum*. There was a quotation from St. Augustine: "The things of which we have charge do not belong to us but to the poor." And from St. Ambrose: "The church has gold, not to hoard away, but to share out and to help those in need." And from St. Jerome: "Whatever the clergy have belongs to the poor, and their houses ought to be common to all." [34]

But this, too, is in the realm of pious exhortation rather than of formal legal definition. Certainly the clergy as well as the poor did have some rights in church property, if only the right to their own support. "He who serves the altar should live of the altar" was an ancient and familiar saying, and one that received a good deal of emphasis in the thirteenth century. But phrases like that of St. Jerome just quoted seemed to deny to the clergy any right to own private property at all, and Gratian devoted a long discussion to the point. He concluded that a cleric could retain ownership of private property but that, if he did so, he could not also draw an income from his church.[35] Joannes Teutonicus disagreed, holding that any cleric could own property unless he had taken a vow of poverty; but although he maintained that a cleric could not legally be deprived of the revenues of his church on the ground that he possessed private means, he also taught that a wealthy cleric who accepted an ecclesiastical income from motives of avarice was guilty of sin.[36] In a rather different spirit Innocent IV taught that a priest who possessed a private fortune had a perfect right to live "of the altar," that is, from the revenues of his church rather than from his own patrimony, and this became the generally accepted view.[37] There was thus a growing emphasis on the right of a priest who served a church to receive due compensation for services rendered, but this line of thought did not lead on to any acceptable definition of the ultimate ownership of the church property that he administered.

The earlier commentaries on the *Decretum* hardly touched on this problem,[38] but three of the major glosses written in the early years of the thirteenth century did take up the question in some detail. The French gloss, *Ecce Vicit Leo*, suggested that ownership, although it could not inhere in any one cleric, might inhere in a corporate group of them, and that perhaps the chapter of the cathedral church could be regarded as owner of all the revenues of the diocese. But this opened up the possibility that everything might fall into the hands of a single surviving member of the cathedral chapter, and this the author of the gloss was not prepared to countenance. He therefore fell back on the suggestion that ownership belonged to God or to the poor. The *Glossa Palatina* mentioned the possibility of regarding the church building as a fictional legal person endowed with ownership, but the author preferred another solution. He thought that, although dominion could not be assigned to any one cleric or to any specific group of them, it could be regarded as inhering in the totality of the clergy considered collectively.[39] Joannes Teutonicus mentioned this solution along with several others. "It is asked who is the owner of things of the Church," he began.

Are the poor called owners? An argument for this is . . . [the passage of St. Jerome quoted above]. It can be said that the Church is owner . . . as a heritage is owner [he had in mind another Roman law analogy here]. Others say that it is God himself. . . . Or say dominion rests with the clergy as the ownership of the things of a community with the citizens.

These last words were the same as those of the *Glossa Palatina.* Finally, Joannes added, "The poor are said to be the owners [of church property] because they are supported from it." [40]

The *Glossa Ordinaria* to the Decretals quoted a number of earlier opinions on the question, but did not advance the argument significantly. A fresh impetus to the whole discussion was provided by Pope Innocent IV. He gave a new significance to the platitude that church property belonged to God or Christ by recalling in this context the Pauline doctrine of the Church as the Mystical Body of Christ. St. Paul over and over again referred to Christ as the head to whom all faithful Christians were joined as members in one body, informed by one spirit. Gifts that were given to Christ might therefore be said to belong to Christ in his Church, in effect to the whole Christian community. This was the teaching of Innocent IV. He wrote:

No prelate, but Christ, has possession and dominion of the things of the Church . . . or the churches have possession, that is to say the community of the faithful which is the body of Christ, the head. They are said to belong to the poor as to sustenance. For the common welfare they are divided among the churches of divers places by authority of the supreme pontiff, and administration of them is conceded to bishops and other prelates.[41]

In this view ownership was vested in the whole community and the poor had a right to support from this common property. Elsewhere Innocent wrote: "The pope and the churches possess all in the name of all men, that thence they may come to the help of all in need." [42] Hostiensis restated and amplified Innocent's arguments. After repeating that dominion rested with the *congregatio fidelium,* the community of the faithful, he went on to analyze St. Jerome's words, "Whatever the clergy have belongs to the poor." *Whatever the clergy have.* That meant whatever they administer, he explained. *Belongs to the poor.* That meant as to sustenance; that is, the poor were to be supported from the goods of the Church. Accordingly, "No one shall call his own what belongs to the Church, that is what is given for the common welfare." And Hostiensis also observed, "Pope and churches hold the goods they have not as their own but as common possessions, that thence they may help all men suffering want." [43]

These views were decisive for the future. Later canonists did not seek to designate one specific owner of church property to the exclusion of all others, but rather to define and harmonize the rights of all the different classes who had some claim on it. In this approach they were again working toward a solution that corresponded closely with the everyday facts of medieval proprietorship. The normal situation in the Middle Ages was that a variety of persons—the serf, the lord of the manor, and his feudal lord in turn—all had different rights in a given tract of land. Henricus de Bohic explained the various rights in church property in a formula that was widely accepted in the fourteenth century:

If you ask to whom ecclesiastical goods are said to belong, here it is said that they belong to the Church. . . . Elsewhere it is said that they belong to God. . . . Elsewhere it is said that they belong to the poor. . . . And again it is said that they belong to the clergy. . . . But Hostiensis [and others] harmonize the above opinions, saying, and I believe rightly, that the Church, that is, the community of the faithful, has dominion over them, and principally Christ as head. What is said of the poor is true as to sustenance, and what is said of the clergy is true as to administration or government, and for this reason clergy are called agents [procuratores], not owners.[44]

This theory of church property would in itself, I think, justify speaking of a canonistic theory of public relief. When the property of the Church was used on behalf of the poor, this was no private charity. The property was public property, its ownership vested in the whole Christian community, its use entrusted to the officers of the Church "for the common welfare" and especially for the sustenance of the poor. There is a widespread misunderstanding implied in phrases like these from a modern work: "The Church in the person of the bishop shouldered the burden of feeding, clothing and sheltering the poor." "This situation was the result of the lack of public assistance." When the bishop helped the poor from ecclesiastical revenues, it was precisely public assistance that he was administering.

The discussion of canonistic theories on property leads on naturally to two central problems of medieval poor relief. The first might be called the theory of charity—the analysis of the attitudes appropriate in a dispenser of alms and a recipient and of the relationship that should exist between them. The second problem is that of administrative machinery—the canonists' teaching concerning the institutional structure through which the relief of the poor was to be effected. These topics will be considered in the next two chapters.

CHAPTER

III Charity

If I have a full stomach and a full purse and I come upon a starving man, ought I to help him? If so, why? And, if there is a whole class of destitute persons in society, ought I to be taxed to support them? And, again, if so, why? The answers are not so entirely self-evident as may at first sight appear. It would hardly do to reply to the first question that a man's benevolent instincts will naturally lead him to help another in distress. It depends rather on the circumstances; the priest and the Levite in the parable found it easier to pass by on the other side of the road. It would be obviously untrue to reply to the second question that the maintenance of the state itself requires that governments protect their weaker citizens. Twentieth-century experience suggests that it is quite possible to organize a state on the basis of exterminating the unproductive or unwanted elements of the population. There are other answers, of course.

Individual devotion to charitable causes is widely recognized as the easiest, and perhaps in the long run the cheapest, method of winning a prominent place in the society pages of the newspapers. And, from the political point of view, at any rate in democratic societies, the poor have votes that may be influenced by handouts. Cynics might find in such considerations intelligible motives for some forms of private and public charity in the twentieth century.

The social worker, in the act of choosing his profession, is presumably committed to the view that the needy should be helped and, nowadays perhaps, to the view that public authorities should assume some part of the burden. For him the main interest in these questions about motivation lies in the fact that the motives of charity are likely to influence the methods of charity. The reasons why we help the poor may help to determine how we help the poor. And, for the student of medieval poor law in particular, this point has special importance, because the whole burden of the criticism most commonly directed against the medieval Church in this sphere is that its theory of charity encouraged a system of poor relief that was not only inefficient but positively pernicious in its effects.

A medieval canonist would have found no difficulty in replying to questions about the motives of charity. His attitude can be summed up in a few scriptural texts that were always on the lips of medieval men when such questions were discussed: "Thou shalt love the Lord thy God with all thy heart, and with all thy soul, . . . and thy neighbour as thyself." "And as ye would that men should do to you, do ye also to them likewise." "Give, and it shall be given unto you. . . . For with the same measure that ye mete withal it shall be measured to you again." And here again the doctrine of the Mystical Body: "So we, being many, are one body in Christ, and every one members one of another." [1] Finally, a text that brings together all the threads of early Christian teaching on charity, the description of the day of judgment in St. Matthew:

Then shall the King say unto them on his right hand, Come, ye blessed of my Father, inherit the kingdom prepared for you from the foundation of the world: For I was an hungred, and ye gave me meat: I was thirsty, and ye gave me drink: I was a stranger, and ye took me in: Naked, and ye clothed me: I was sick, and ye visited me: I was in prison, and ye came unto me. Then shall the righteous answer him, saying, Lord, when saw we thee an hungred, and fed thee? or thirsty, and gave thee drink? When saw we thee a stranger, and took thee in? or naked, and clothed thee? Or when saw we thee sick, or in prison, and came unto thee? And the King shall answer and say unto them, Verily I say unto you, Inasmuch as ye have done it unto one of the least of these my brethren, ye have done it unto me.[2]

There is, evidently enough, an element of self-interest in the Christian doctrine of charity, even in its scriptural form. A man was urged to give alms generously with the assurance that his action would be pleasing to God and would merit a heavenly reward. In the Middle Ages, when it was a question of raising funds for charitable purposes, this aspect might be emphasized for obvious tactical reasons. Perhaps the best example from a canonistic source is the letter of authorization for collectors on behalf of charitable institutions, approved by the Fourth Lateran Council and included in the Decretals of Gregory IX. It begins like this:

Since, as the Apostle says, we shall all stand before the tribunal of Christ to be received according as we have borne ourselves in the body, whether good or ill, it behooves us to anticipate the day of harvest with works of great mercy, and, for the sake of things eternal, to sow on earth what we should gather in heaven, the Lord returning it with increased fruit.[3]

It is this self-regarding element that is the focal point of all the criticism of medieval charity. It may be argued simply on moral grounds that medieval almsgiving lacked genuine altruism. But this is at least debatable. In the theory implied by the scriptural texts and worked out in detail by the canonists and theologians, almsgiving was conceived of as an act of justice or an act of love, but not as a matter of sentimental impulse. A man's duty was to love God and to love his neighbor because God so willed. The neighbor might be personally repugnant—the poor often are—but he was none the less entitled to affectionate respect and help in need for the sake of Christ. A man who conforms his actions to the will of God in the knowledge that this is for the good of his

own soul may be described as selfish; but the world would go
on well enough if everyone practiced that kind of selfishness.

The more important criticism of the medieval theory of charity
is concerned with its practical rather than its moral implications.
It is argued that the emphasis on the intrinsic virtue of almsgiving
led to a complete neglect of the effect of the alms on the recipient,
and that this in turn caused nearly all the resources available for
the relief of the poor to be squandered in "indiscriminate charity,"
which, we are usually given to understand, was far worse than no
charity at all.

This argument was advanced most trenchantly in the nineteenth
century by Albert Emminghaus,[4] and it evoked a sharp reply from
the great medieval scholar, Cardinal Ehrle, who produced a long
series of quotations from the church Fathers urging the need for
discretion in almsgiving.[5] Ehrle seems to have had the best of the
verbal duel, but his arguments apparently did not really convince
subsequent writers on the problem. Sir William Ashley, whose very
able work has still, after more than sixty years, not been supplanted
as the standard account of medieval poor relief in England,
conceded that "so far as the *theory* of almsgiving is concerned, the
Mediaeval Church was free from the fault that has been imputed
to it." [6] But the whole tone of Ashley's writing implied the opposite
point of view. His pages are studded with phrases like "the
haphazard charity which current religious notions encouraged,"
and with views like this, ". . . the predominant motive in making
charitable bequests was to secure an advantage in the next world.
. . . There can be no question that such almsgiving was bound
to be haphazard and demoralizing." He complained that there
was an essential weakness in even the harshest of medieval vagrancy
laws in that they did not prohibit almsgiving to the impotent poor,
and added, "With the current ideas as to the meritorious character
of alms, it would have seemed impious to forbid Christians to
earn the reward of charity." [7] All these observations seem to imply
misgivings about the theory as well as the practice of medieval
charity. As for the practice itself, Ashley was scathing. The kindest
thing he wrote about any form of medieval charity was his
comment on the practice of providing dowries to enable poor girls

to marry. This, he thought, "could do little harm." [8] For the most part he was indignant about "the mischief of indiscriminate charity." "The reckless distribution of doles cannot have failed to exercise a pauperizing influence," he maintained. The monasteries were "centres of pauperization," and "the crying need was to put an end to the old pauperizing system of indiscriminate charity." [9]

In discussing the legal status of the poor I have already referred to the great difference that existed between the implicit assumptions of medieval society concerning the relief of poverty and the assumptions that commended themselves to the society of the Industrial Revolution. The contrast is indeed so obvious that it may seem futile to labor the point further. But the problem of discrimination in medieval charity can hardly be studied satisfactorily unless the contrast is explicitly stated and constantly borne in mind, since nearly all previous discussions of the subject have been influenced by the preconceptions of early industrial society. Much of the best writing on the history of charity was done in the latter part of the nineteenth century, the main works on which Ashley relied as well as his own book. At that time the basic principles of the Poor Law act of 1834 were still widely accepted. It was assumed that if a man was destitute he was probably an idle lout who deserved punishment. It was further assumed, apparently, that all working people were idle louts at heart who would not work if public or private relief for the destitute could be had without the most bitter humiliations and hardships. To men influenced by such principles there seemed a kind of outrageous perversity in the naïve medieval view that the kindest way of dealing with a hungry man was to feed him. This they called "pauperization." We have still to consider what the law of the Church and the doctrines of the canonists did say about indiscriminate charity, but we may observe as a preliminary that, even if we find in them nothing at all about workhouse tests or the "principle of less eligibility," this need not lead us automatically to accept the strictures of Ashley and his contemporaries. It has become fashionable, and facile, to decry the rather shallow rationalism of our Victorian great-grandfathers, but one may still be permitted a little indignation about those scientific radicals who

made the nineteenth-century English poor law, those last dim sparks
of the Enlightenment, so implacably resolved on being rational
that, in this matter at least, they could never find time to be
reasonable. Indeed, it has seemed to some people that the nineteenth
century, far more that the thirteenth, provides the classic example
of a radically defective theory of charity producing pernicious
results in actual administrative practice.

A convenient approach to the canonists' doctrine of charity is to
consider it under two aspects: first, its treatment of the benefactor,
his obligations and proper attitude to the poor, and then its
treatment of the beneficiary, especially the circumstances and
qualifications that rendered a man eligible for charitable assistance
in canonistic theory. Such a treatment will at least emphasize that
there were two sides to the canonists' teaching. Like the authors
of modern books on social casework, they were aware that an
adequate theory of poor relief had to concern itself with the conduct
and attitudes of the administrators of charity as well as with the
qualifications and claims of applicants for it. As Guido de Baysio
wrote, to be regarded as truly virtuous an act of charity had to
be consistent with right reason, which meant that the effect of
the gift had to be considered from the point of view of both the
giver and the receiver.[10]

The preoccupation with the effect of almsgiving on the soul of
the benefactor, which certainly did exist, sometimes led the
canonists into elaborate disquisitions on problems that may seem
tedious and irrelevant to the modern mind. One that particularly
engaged their attention was whether a man could give alms from
property illicitly acquired, and also whether the Church could
collect tithes—ecclesiastical taxation—from such property. Such
issues are not altogther dead. One can still occasionally hear heated
arguments about the morality of financing church charities by mild
forms of gambling, and several years ago the propriety of taxing
illicit gains was debated with some vigor in Washington in connection with a law requiring bookmakers to pay a registration tax,
although their business was illegal. But, for the modern student
of charitable organization and poor relief, such problems, if they
arise at all, are peripheral ones. For the medieval canonists they

were of central importance. There was some indecisive discussion in the *Decretum* about gambling gains: Could they be given to the poor or did they have to be returned to the loser? [11] But more important and more straightforward was the case of theft. A thief certainly could not perform a meritorious act by giving alms to the poor; his plain duty was to make restitution to the victim. Although the canonists conceded that a man in extreme want could take what he needed without himself incurring guilt, they did not condone Robin Hood tactics of stealing from the rich to give to the poor. This was called a suggestion of the devil.[12] The *Summa Parisiensis* put forward the engaging suggestion that, although a thief could not derive spiritual benefit by distributing his loot to the poor, perhaps the real owner did.[13] Apparently the author could not bear to think of the virtue of the act being lost entirely. But this idea found no support. A somewhat more subtle point arose in connection with money that was acquired illicitly but not by actual theft. Stephanus Tornacensis argued that a thief could derive no spiritual benefit from giving alms, since they were given against the will of the real owner; but a prostitute could properly give alms since she did acquire possession with the consent of the owner, even though illicitly.[14] This led on to the general principle, formulated by the thirteenth-century canonists, that almsgiving even from illicitly acquired property was meritorious, providing that legal ownership had passed to the donor and there was no injured party to claim restitution.[15]

In reading some of the later argumentation one feels at times that it might have been as well if they had left it at that. In fact, the principle merely provided a springboard for more complicated arguments assessing the moral value of alms given from property acquired in nearly all conceivable circumstances. Guido de Baysio, for instance, devoted the most complex casuistry to the problem. After the first obvious distinction between goods licitly acquired and those illicitly acquired, he distinguished further within the second category. Goods acquired illicitly belonged to someone or to no one. To explain the latter class he cited the example of a bishop who went out hunting. The game he took would be acquired illicitly, not because it was taken from someone else, but because bishops were forbidden to hunt by canon law. All the same, having acquired it, he could properly bestow it as alms. If goods were acquired illicitly from an owner they were taken either against his will (in which case no alms could be given from them), or without his knowledge (and again no alms could be given), or by his handing them over in some transaction. In the last eventuality there was a further distinction. The transaction might be such as to involve the giver only in moral turpitude, or the receiver only, or both the giver and the receiver. There is a certain air of timelessness in Guido's examples of transactions involving the receiver in turpitude. He mentioned usurers, lawyers who charged immense and unreasonable fees, doctors who cheated the sick out of their money when there was nothing seriously wrong with them, and corrupt government officials. None of these could do their souls any good by giving alms from their gains. And so the argument meandered on and on, wandering tortuously through a jungle of distinctions and subdistinctions.[16]

It is this kind of passage that is likely to make a modern investigator impatient with medieval theories of charity. There seems to be no evidence of real concern for the poor at all, only an elaborate explanation of the circumstances in which a donor could expect to get full value in spiritual coin for alms given, and when not. Such an impression is not altogether just. The canonists devoted just as much detailed discussion in other contexts to the position of the beneficiary as they did here to the ethics of the benefactor. One needs to bear in mind, too, all their discussions on the theory of property which issued in such a clear and trenchant doctrine on the just rights of the poor. All the arguments on these different topics hung together in a pattern and the pattern has to be judged as a whole. Moreover, it is not a pattern imposed by the mind of the historian on heterogeneous fragments of unrelated material —always a danger in this kind of research—but a pattern that was quite apparent to the canonists themselves. That is to say, when discussing some abstract problem concerning the theory of property, they would give references to other contexts which explained the practical implications of their doctrine in the sphere of charity; and so too, in discussing the obligation of almsgiving, they would refer back to the theory of property which supported their views.

The canonists' views on the circumstances in which a man was bound to give have already been considered. The canonists also had a great deal to say about the manner of the giving. It has often been maintained that medieval thought, or even Christian thought in general, on the motives for helping the poor is clouded by a confusion between the virtue of ascetic renunciation and the virtue of compassionate charity; and certainly the two elements often coexist in an act of Christian almsgiving.[17] It is interesting, therefore, that the canonists drew quite a clear distinction between the methods appropriate in the disposal of goods for the first reason, and those recommended when the second motive was dominant. When a man wished to renounce all worldly property to enter the religious life—the ascetic motive—it was proper for him to give away all his goods at once, to strip himself of all earthly impediments. But when a man was simply concerned with fulfilling his obligation of charity toward his neighbors, he was required to dispose of the available property with discretion, a little at a time, so that as many as possible could be helped. "Discretion is to be observed," wrote Rufinus, closely following the words of the *Decretum* itself, ". . . so that not everything is poured out at once, except when a man wishes to strip himself of all worldly responsibilities, nakedly to serve God." [18] Joannes Teutonicus also observed that a man ought not to pour forth all his goods at once, and explained in another context that the smaller the sums doled out, the more people could be helped. For the same reason, only plain and simple food was to be offered to the poor, not luxuries.[19] Again, Hostiensis wrote that generosity on the grandest scale was a noble virtue, but added that a man who poured out his wealth everywhere and without discrimination was not to be accounted noble. Rather he was a spendthrift and a fool.[20]

Above all, the canonists insisted that for a work of charity to be a meritorious act, pleasing to God, it had to be inspired by a right attitude to God and to one's neighbor. St. Augustine used a slightly odd-sounding phrase that was quoted in the *Decretum* to describe this right attitude. "Who would give alms in due order ought to begin with himself, and first give to himself." [21] According to the *Glossa Ordinaria*, this meant that the almsgiver must first purify his own heart, "for a man who loves iniquity hates his own soul." To show charity to himself meant, therefore, to turn away from wickedness. A man intent on evil could not please God by giving freely, and certainly could not gain a license to go on sinning by lavish almsgiving.[22] As for the attitude to one's neighbor, Gratian quoted the words of St. Paul, "God loves a cheerful giver." And of St. Ambrose, "It is not enough to do good unless the act flows from a good source, that is a good will." And St. Augustine was quoted again, "There are two kinds of almsgiving, one of the heart, one of money. . . . The alms of love are sufficient in a man without worldly substance, but what is given in a physical sense, if it is given without a loving heart, is altogether insufficient." [23] The *Glossa Ordinaria* maintained that to give alms without any charity in the heart, simply to get rid of an importunate beggar, was not only without merit but actually sinful. (Guido de Baysio explained that the sin did not consist in the act of giving, which was good in itself, but in showering abuse on the beggar.[24]) Similarly it was held sinful to give alms from motives of vainglory. The canonistic doctrine in this matter was summed up in the teaching of Guido de Baysio that almsgiving should be generous and should conform to the three principles of justice, order, and right intention. Justice—the almsgiver should give from his own justly acquired property; order—he should establish a proper order of righteousness in his own soul; right intention—he should give from motives of true charity, not merely to avoid embarrassment or win worldly praise.[25]

When this theory of charity was generally accepted, there was naturally little tendency to assume that the acceptance of alms was in itself degrading or corrupting as was very commonly assumed in later systems of poor relief. To a medieval man a meritorious act of charity was good from all points of view. The one who gave displayed the virtue of generosity, and the one who received displayed the virtue of humility. Such an attitude might indeed seem to open the way to all the abuses of "indiscriminate charity," yet, even in the passages considered thus far, which are concerned mainly with the ethical position of the benefactor, there are hints that care and discretion in the distribution of alms were enjoined. There is much more on this same theme in the discussions on the various classes of applicants for charity.

Apparently the reason that Cardinal Ehrle's compilation of theological texts urging discrimination in almsgiving has not proved altogether convincing to subsequent writers is that the quotations appear as mere obiter dicta, fragments taken out of context, rather than as detailed analyses of a serious problem. Thus the Webbs wrote, with a reference to Ehrle, "The diligent student can pick out all down the centuries, from the more statesmanlike Catholic writers, isolated sentences pointing to the duty of practical wisdom in almsgiving. . . ." But the Webbs made it clear that they did not attach any great importance to the fact, for they at once added, "But the overwhelming tendency of regarding alms as an act of piety, like fasting and prayer, principally from the standpoint of the state of mind of the giver, was in the direction of dismissing all considerations with regard to the character of the recipient." The criticism implied by the phrase "isolated sentences" is simply not applicable to the canonists, and it is simply not true that they displayed an overwhelming tendency to consider almsgiving from the point of view of the giver to the exclusion of other considerations.[26] They discussed the problem of discrimination in charity on innumerable occasions, in great detail, and with a full realization that they were debating an issue of major importance. There is probably more writing in canonistic sources on this particular point than on any other problem in the field of poor relief.

The issue arose for the canonists both as a practical problem of relief administration and as a theoretical problem of harmonizing the discordant texts of the *Decretum*. This was one instance when Gratian left a difficult task of interpretation to his successors, for he himself hesitated between two contrary opinions, at one point urging openhanded generosity to all, and at another point insisting on the need for cautious discrimination in the bestowal of alms. There were many relevant texts scattered through the *Decretum* which were brought into play by the canonists,[27] but the argument mainly turned on Gratian's citations from three of the early church Fathers, St. John Chrysostom, St. Ambrose, and St. Augustine. St. John Chrysostom appears in the *Decretum* as the champion of unhesitating help to all in need, St. Ambrose and St. Augustine as advocates of careful discrimination. The task for the canonists was to decide which was the right policy, and how far the apparently contradictory texts of the Fathers could be reconciled with one another.

In introducing the critical text of St. John Chrysostom, Gratian commented: "In hospitality there is to be no regard for persons, but we ought to welcome indifferently all for whom our resources suffice." [28] The citation from the saint himself opened with a resounding blast against that procedure of persecution by inquisition which has always attracted some poor relief administrators. "Let us have no more of this ridiculous, diabolical, peremptory prying," wrote St. John Chrysostom. He went on to explain that if a stranger represented himself to be a priest, then he was indeed to be examined before the faithful received the sacraments from him and contributed to his support; but if a poor man simply asked for food because he was in need he was to be helped without any inquisition.[29] The proposition that a stranger calling himself a priest should be carefully examined was always approved by the canonists; it was the second part of the argument that provoked discussion. The *Glossa Ordinaria*, for instance, observed that, according to this text, alms were to be given to all indiscriminately, and cited half a dozen other passages that supported this point of view, but then added half a dozen more that said just the opposite.

The arguments against St. John Chrysostom's position were set out most systematically in *Distinctio* 86 of the *Decretum*, which developed a whole theory of the "deserving poor" and the "undeserving poor"—to use the terminology of a later age. Here Gratian himself seems to have adopted a point of view contrary to the one already quoted. He was discussing in this part of his work the various qualities essential in a bishop, and at this point he came to the quality of *liberalitas*—generosity. A bishop was to be generous to the poor, he observed, but then added: "In this generosity due measure is to be applied both of things and of persons; of things,

that not everything is to be bestowed on one but on various individuals, . . . of persons, that we give first to the just, then to
sinners, to whom, nevertheless, we are forbidden to give not as
men but as sinners." [30] The somewhat obscure phrase, "not as men
but as sinners," was promptly explained by a series of quotations
from St. Augustine, in which the saint inveighed against those
who wasted their resources on such followers of reprehensible
professions as fortunetellers, gladiators, actors and actresses, and
prostitutes. St. Augustine's complaint was that people gave to such
folk precisely for the sake of what was most evil in them: "Those
who give to gladiators give not to the man but to his evil art.
For if he was only a man and not a gladiator, you would not
give. . . ." [31] This is what Gratian meant by writing that it was
forbidden to give to sinners not as men but as sinners. The *Glossa
Ordinaria* explained that to give to members of vile professions for
exercising their arts was wrong, but that such people were not to
be refused charitable assistance if they were in real need. "The
vice is not to be nourished, but nature is to be sustained," Joannes
wrote. [32]

Immediately after these observations of St. Augustine, Gratian
presented a lengthy series of extracts from St. Ambrose, taken
mostly from his *De Officiis*. These chapters really form the back-
bone of the *Decretum*'s teaching on poor relief, and Gratian could
not have chosen better, for Ambrose was not only a revered theologian but also, as Bishop of Milan in the fourth century, one
of the greatest practical poor relief administrators of all time. His
De Officiis was a book of guidance for the clergy in the fulfilling
of their pastoral duties and, in the sections quoted, he was explaining
to them how they should discriminate among the different classes
of poor folk who sought assistance.

In the first place, those who were faithful Christians were to be
helped. It was a great disgrace if any of these fell into want or
affliction without being succored. Then, regard was to be paid to
age and sickness and to the sense of shame that would affect those
of good birth. The old and sick who could not seek food by their
own labor were to be helped more readily than others, and also
those who fell from riches into want, especially if it was through

no fault of their own. Again, a man had a special obligation to support his own parents.[33] In a passage that was not included in the *Decretum,* but was known to the canonists and quoted in the *Glossa Ordinaria,* Ambrose wrote that a man ought to love first God, then his parents, then his children, then the other members of his household, and then strangers.[34] The idea that "charity begins at home," that it should spread out as it were in concentric circles, and in the first place to one's family and close associates, was deeply rooted in medieval theory and practice. It was always conceded, for instance, that a priest could properly use the property of his church to assist his parents if they were in need, even though he was frequently reminded that such property was not his own, but a public trust.[35] And Martinus de Fano, at the beginning of the thirteenth century, produced a complex little treatise setting out in detail precisely what degrees of relationship entitled a person to claim maintenance from other members of his family.[36] The canonists even invented a sort of legal conundrum out of Ambrose's texts on this point. A man was especially bound to help faithful Christians and he was also specially bound to help his own parents. But what if his father was an infidel? Was his obligation greater to the father or to an outsider who was a good Christian? Petrus Manducator, a theologian of the late twelfth century, dismissed the question as nebulous nonsense—"murky water in the clouds of the air," he called it; but the canonists, while quoting Petrus' opinion apparently as a bon mot that had gone the round of the schools, discussed the issue solemnly enough and usually came down on the side of the erring father. When both men were in equal need, family responsibilities took preference over other considerations; if, however, one of them was in a more desperate plight than the other, the more urgent case was to be helped.[37] It is generally true of the canonists' discussions that, though they would consider a wide variety of factors to be taken into account in the distribution of alms, the degree of need in the individual applicant was always ultimately the decisive factor.

The various texts of St. Ambrose did not actually exclude any class of undeserving poor from the reception of alms, but merely established an order of preference among the applicants. Rigid exclusion was suggested, however, by another text of St. Augustine, quoted in a different part of the *Decretum*, which was of fundamental importance for the canonists' theory of poor relief. "One who spares is not always a friend," wrote St. Augustine, "nor one who strikes a foe. It is better to love with severity than to deceive with lenience. It is more useful to take bread away from a hungry man, if when he was sure of food he neglected justice, than to give bread to him so that, being led astray, he may rejoice in injustice." [38] This is another example of a passage that acquired a significance in canon law rather different from its meaning in the original context. In the letter from which it was taken, Augustine was defending measures of coercion adopted by the imperial government of his day against the sect of Donatist heretics. His real theme was the suppression of heresy, not the relief of poverty. But the words about denying bread to a man who would be led into injustice if sure of his food seemed to the canonists to provide an essential link in their theory of poor relief, and was frequently quoted in their discussions on the administration of charity. The *Glossa Ordinaria* to the *Decretum*, for instance, cited Augustine's words to prove that relief should not be given to able-bodied idle beggars: "The Church ought not to provide for a man who is able to work, . . . for strong men, sure of their food without work, often do neglect justice." [39] In this same context, Joannes Teutonicus cited the Roman law that a man able to work, who accepted public relief, was to be treated as a criminal and condemned to slavery. Poverty as such was not a crime in the eyes of the canonists, but certainly willful idleness was. Joannes also insisted that alms should be given only to genuinely needy cases; to give to others, he wrote, was mere squandering.[40]

In considering these views it is important to bear in mind that there was no mass unemployment in the high Middle Ages such as we have seen in modern times. There must have been individual hard cases where a poor man held no land and could find no work at hand for a time, but, as a general rule, it was a fair assumption that a healthy man could support himself if he chose to work. The medieval almoner was not normally faced with the routine

problem of a modern social worker, to determine whether a man
was unable to find work or unwilling to look for it. This must
have simplified the task of discrimination when there was any
real will to discriminate.

The dialectical problem, of course, was to reconcile the texts
urging discrimination in charity with the teaching of St. John
Chrysostom that alms should be given to all without inquiry or
discrimination. Although the problem was often discussed there
was little real difference of opinion among the canonists. The
main lines of the generally accepted solution were already laid
down in the *Summa* of Rufinus, one of the first major commentaries
on the *Decretum*. After citing the authorities against indiscriminate
charity, Rufinus wrote:

By all this it is shown that we ought not to show ourselves generous
indiscriminately to all who come. But it should be known that in providing hospitality these four things are to be considered: the quality of
the one seeking alms, the resources of the giver, the cause of the request,
and the amount requested. The quality of the one asking—whether he
is honest or dishonest; the resources of the one giving—whether they can
suffice for all or only for some; the cause of the request—whether a man
asks only for food for the love of God or says he is sent as a preacher and
therefore claims a due stipend from you; the amount requested—whether
it is excessive or reasonable. If the one who asks is dishonest, and especially
if he is able to seek his food by his own labor and neglects to do so, so that
he chooses rather to beg or steal, without doubt nothing is to be given
to him, but he is to be corrected . . . unless perchance he is close to
perishing from want, for then, if we have anything we ought to give
indifferently to all such. . . . But if the one who asks is honest, you
ought to give to all of this sort if the resources available suffice. . . .
But if you cannot give to all asking of you then you should give first to
those close to you; in this case the authorities on discrimination in giving
are to be applied.[41]

Rufinus concluded that a man claiming to be a priest was to be
carefully examined, and that requests for excessive sums were to
be refused. The essential points in his arguments were the special
provision for cases of extreme need and the distinction between
the measures to be applied when abundant supplies were available

for all applicants and those appropriate when supplies were limited. Raymundus de Pennaforte, compiler of the Gregorian Decretals, made the same distinctions in his *Summa Iuris:*

Either you have enough for all or not. In the first case you ought to give to all indiscriminately, . . . and this is true except when by being made sure of his food a man would neglect justice, for in that case "it is more useful to take away bread from the needy, etc." . . . except when he is dying of hunger, for then he ought to be fed however much he may neglect justice. In the second case, namely, when you have not enough to suffice for all, then you ought to consider nine things,[42]

and he went on with a discussion of the proper order of preference based on St. Ambrose's texts. Joannes Teutonicus, in his *Glossa Ordinaria,* put forward very similar principles,[43] and the later canonists who dealt with this theme merely elaborated the same arguments without significantly changing their content. Henricus de Bohic, in mid-fourteenth century, began by distinguishing between those in extreme want and others. All those in the first category were to be helped. Of the rest, some were "ribald folk" who played dice all day and some were not. The ribald folk were to be refused. In dealing with the others, one either had enough for all, or not—and the argument went on from there in the usual way.[44] The essential principles were always the same. If there was not enough for all, St. Ambrose's system of preferences was to be carefully applied. If there was enough for all, St. John Chrysostom's principle of indiscriminate aid could be adopted, but with one exception, that alms should not be given to the willfully idle and vicious who would be harmed more than helped by readily available charity; but even they were to be fed if their need was desperate.

Some of the glosses of the thirteenth century introduced an apparently harsh note into their discussions with the quotation of another Roman law dictum: "It is in the public interest that the undeserving should labor in want." The phrase was applied by Hostiensis and Bernardus Parmensis to the case of an excommunicated priest, when the question at issue was whether the bishop had any duty to support such a man; and, again, to the case of a spendthrift who fell into want as a result of his own extravagance; and to the case of an unbeneficed priest who had lost all his private fortune through gambling.[45] But the canonists were not arguing that such misguided individuals should be left to starve, only that there was no reason why they should not earn their bread in the sweat of their brows. Both Bernardus and Hostiensis, after observing that the undeserving should labor in want, added that if a man was really destitute he should be given alms. Canonistic teaching did not exclude anyone from receiving assistance on the grounds of past wickedness or folly. Even an infidel or an excommunicate was to be cared for, though, if the resources available were not abundant, he might have to take his turn at the end of the line.[46] The only ground for refusal was the presumption that almsgiving would encourage future wickedness by making possible an idle and vicious way of life.

But, of course, this was the argument that was always used in later centuries to justify deterrent systems of poor relief. It may seem, therefore, that I have begun by inveighing against nineteenth-century doctrines and have finished by proving that the medieval canonists taught exactly the same things. The real difference is that the canonists never advocated any policies that would have deterred the genuinely needy from seeking help. They insisted on the need for discrimination in dealing with the poor, and there seems no sufficient reason for supposing that all medieval almoners ignored their plain canonical duty in this matter. But the rough and ready methods available would hardly have excluded the more resourceful sort of professional beggar with faked sores and ingeniously twisted limbs, and no one doubts that medieval administration erred in the direction of laxity rather than of undue stringency. There is a brief comment of Guido de Baysio that seems relevant here. Writing on St. John Chrysostom's text in favor of indiscriminate charity, he observed that it applied only to "day-to-day" alms, not "premeditated" alms.[47] That is to say, a man could not be expected to investigate every appeal individually, and he ought not to deny to the needy the sums he could give away on a day-to-day basis for fear that his generosity would sometimes be abused. But, when he was contemplating some major endowment, he had a serious responsibility to see that his money was laid out wisely.

Every student of poor relief administration knows that there are some cases where prompt and generous assistance does more harm than good. The medieval canonists knew it as well as anyone else. The point is that the nineteenth-century reformers assumed that such cases were normal, typical of human nature in general, so they based their whole theory and practice on the denial of relief unless it was accompanied by harsh deterrent conditions. The thirteenth-century canonists knew these cases existed, but regarded them as abnormalities, associated with a special type of moral perversity. They taught that it was proper to deny alms to such individuals when they were known, but not that all charitable activity should be regulated as though its principal purpose was to exclude the undeserving rather than to help the deserving. They deprecated the squandering of large sums in "indiscriminate charity," but countenanced a certain open-handedness in day-to-day almsgiving. The canonists must have known that some individuals would abuse such charity, but it never seems to have occurred to them that it could exercise any corrupting influence on society as a whole, an assumption that was often taken for granted in later theories. It was not that they based their doctrines on a romantically rosy view of human nature. No institution has been less afflicted with that delusion that the Catholic Church, and lawyers as a class are not given to undue romanticism. Nor is it true that the canonists failed to reflect on the problems of discrimination in charity. The fact is that, having reflected at some length, they simply did not reach the conclusion that deterrent and punitive measures were either necessary or desirable as normal features of poor law policy. The canonists' attitude is well summed up in the words of Joannes Teutonicus: "In case of doubt it is better to do too much than to do nothing at all." [48]

If we were now to ask the obvious question—who was right, the thirteenth-century lawyers or the nineteenth-century administrators?—we should be posing the central issue in a fashion that

virtually prohibits any intelligent study of it. There is little
point in trying to decide whether thirteenth-century theories or
nineteenth-century theories more closely resembled modern
theories on poor relief. The only sensible question for a medieval
historian to consider is whether the thirteenth-century doctrines
were tolerably well adapted to the social and economic environment
of the thirteenth century itself. Certainly, in approaching that
question, we cannot ignore the argument that unregulated charity
is always and of necessity a pauperizing influence, inimical to the
real interests of the poor themselves. The famous poor law report
of 1834 may not be convincing; it was an outrageously biased
document. But the records of the Charity Organization Movement
later in the nineteenth century provide more impressive evidence.
Organizers like Sir Charles Loch in England or Mary Richmond
in America were humane people with vast practical experience
of social casework, and they were utterly convinced that charitable
help to the poor, unless most carefully canalized, was positively
baneful in its effects.

The root of the matter is surely this. Whether a given system
of poor relief will exercise a corrupting influence on society depends
at least as much on the structure and mores of the society as on
the precise organization of the charity. Above all it depends on
the social and economic stability of the lowest-paid laboring
classes who are most likely to fall into destitution. Now the typical
problem of the nineteenth century was that of a rootless urban
proletariat, swarming in filthy slums, often without religion and
without family solidarity, a proletariat corrupted moreover by
unpredictable spells of compulsory idleness in times of bad trade.
It is easy enough to believe that among men so situated many
would lose all inclination to work if work could be avoided, and
would abuse any charity that could be abused. The poor relief
administrators of the time could not help but be aware of the
fact. Their great failure of insight on the practical level lay in
their blank inability to comprehend that the poor devils to whom
they lectured about thrift and frugality were often reduced to
destitution, quite regardless of their own virtue or lack of it, by
social factors over which they had no control whatsoever. The

failure that one sometimes encounters on the level of historical interpretation lay in the assumption that experience of such a society provided absolute criteria by which to judge the poor relief arrangements of all others.

The canonists were dealing with an entirely different type of social environment, an environment that produced both a different kind of poverty and a different attitude to charity. I am referring now only to the high Middle Ages and especially to the thirteenth century itself. Circumstances changed considerably in the late fourteenth and the fifteenth centuries, and the changes that occurred then account for the relative failure of ecclesiastical poor relief arrangements at the end of the Middle Ages. But, in the thirteenth century, there existed a stable and, by preindustrial standards, rather prosperous society in which the vast majority of the poorer people were peasant farmers, living in small villages and rooted to their own land. There was no mass unemployment, as we have observed, and the vast majority of cases of real destitution must have arisen from personal vicissitudes: a crippling accident making it impossible for a peasant to work his land, or a long illness, or the impotence of old age. There must have been many cases, too, where a family breadwinner died leaving a widow with a family of small children. The average expectation of life in thirteenth-century England was only a little more than thirty years, and the canonists were always particularly concerned about the protection of widows and orphans.

Sometimes the customary manorial law of land tenure and inheritance offered some protection to the villein and his family against the more common vicissitudes of life. In a group of manors studied by F. M. Page a kind of primitive "social security" existed for those who became too old or weak to render the services due from their land and had no sons to do so. In those circumstances the tenancy of the holding was transferred to another villein, but the old tenant was assigned the produce of part of the land, usually half a dozen acres with a cottage and garden, which was worked by the incoming tenant. When a villein died leaving a widow and children, the widow succeeded to her husband's land without paying the usual inheritance tax to the lord. She held the land until

she died or remarried, when it passed on to the next heir, who
was the youngest, not the oldest, son, presumably because the
youngest was the one least likely to be able to fend for himself.
After describing these arrangements, Miss Page observed that

. . . it is difficult to over-rate the customary land law as a method of
poor relief which, contrary to the monastic method of indiscriminate
charity and the modern dole, made a strong attempt to remove the root
cause of poverty and establish the poor man in a position of self-respecting,
though only partial, independence, with the stimulus to make some effort
for his own support.[49]

A state of need that was only temporary was often met without
recourse to organized charities. Family loyalties were strong and
neighbors were often banded together in guilds (religious fra-
ternities in the villages as well as craft guilds in the towns). The
part played by the medieval guilds in the general relief of poverty
has sometimes been exaggerated, but they did commonly provide
help for their own impoverished members, and they must have
absorbed much fortuitous distress that in a less organic society
would have produced cases for the public relief authorities. This
state of affairs was quite in keeping with the canonists' doctrine
that a man's first obligation of charity was toward his own family
and his close associates. The medieval canonists were entirely in
harmony with the pioneers of the Charity Organization Movement
on at least this one matter, though they approached it from a
different point of view. The canonists stressed the primary obligation of a man to relieve want in his own immediate circle. The
Charity Organization Movement insisted on the duty of a person
in need to seek help from his family and neighbors before turning
for assistance to public relief and organized charities.

Again, the medieval peasant lived under the eye of a parish
priest, his whole day-to-day life profoundly influenced by a religion
that emphasized the virtue of charity indeed, but that also taught,
"If a man will not work, neither shall he eat." Certainly, if a
peasant failed to do the required work on his lord's land he would
be reminded of his obligation very promptly by a steward's cudgel
laid unofficially across his shoulders or, more properly, by a formal

summons to the manor court and a sharp fine. And if he failed to work on his own land his family would come to lack the bare necessities of life, while the burden of feeding them would probably fall in the first place on relatives and neighbors. Such conduct would obviously evoke extreme disapproval from the whole little community that formed the medieval peasant's world. Altogether there must have existed the most intense social pressures impelling a man to work at least enough to support himself and his dependents. Obviously, some worked harder than others and, as in all ages, some prospered more than others; and obviously too there were occasional misfits, the village idiot or the village rogue, who were unable or unwilling to sustain the give-and-take of community life and who might wander away to become a burden on the available charitable resources. But, considering all the circumstances, it seems downright nonsense to suggest that the possibility of getting a free meal at some monastery halfway across the country could have exercised a demoralizing influence on the average thirteenth-century villager.

Indeed, when we bear in mind the realities of medieval life, it may seem that even the more notorious apparent abuses of charity were relatively harmless, or even perhaps helpful in that particular historical context. The form of charity that above all others aroused Ashley's indignation was the custom of providing a feast for the poor folk who came to pray for the soul of a benefactor at his funeral or its anniversary. But poor men in the Middle Ages, even those above the level of destitution, lived hard, monotonous lives with dull, unvaried diets providing little more than the bare necessities for subsistence. I am sometimes tempted to think that, in those circumstances, for a rich man to arrange that his poor neighbors should have their fill of good food and good drink at least once in the year was a most imaginative and worthy form of charity, profiting greatly the bodies and minds of the beneficiaries, and, let us hope, the soul of the benefactor too.

But I fear that a medieval canonist would not have taken such a liberal view, and unfortunately occasional feasts do not provide any effective answer to the long-term problems of poverty. Of course, the vast majority of charitable funds available in the Middle

Ages were not employed in that way. When a medieval man wished to make a really substantial bequest to charity, he almost invariably chose to endow a church or a charitable institution. It will be necessary, therefore, to consider next the canon law relating to the administration of ecclesiastical and institutional poor relief.

CHAPTER

IV   *Institutions*

Thus far we have been considering the underlying principles, essentially moral principles, on which the canonists' treatment of poor law problems was based. We have now to turn to the law governing the institutions through which poor relief was administered. Here it seems especially important to consider the functions of the medieval parish, because this theme has been rather neglected in the standard histories of charity, and also because the parish was to assume a position of central importance in the later tradition of English poor law.

In discussing the canonists' theory of church property I suggested that their teachings implied a theory of public poor relief dispensed by ecclesiastical authorities. The obvious questions arise whether the canonists defined any such system in more concrete terms by assigning specific poor relief responsibilities to administrators of ecclesiastical revenues in the dioceses and parishes, and, further, whether such a system really did work in actual administrative practice. These questions involve controversial issues, and the answers to them are of crucial importance in any assessment of medieval poor relief arrangements as a whole. Private charity and privately endowed charitable institutions, encouraged by the doctrine of the Church on property and its obligations, did play a major part in medieval poor relief, but such efforts have

commonly been criticized as indiscriminate and "haphazard." It
has been argued that the indiscriminate charity which was condoned
could hardly have exercised any demoralizing influence on society
as a whole, but it may still be urged that charity of this sort is
inadequate and ineffective, even though not positively harmful.
If, however, all this voluntary effort was supplemented by a
system of parish relief, administered by parish priests who must
have known every detail of the family circumstances of their
parishioners, the charge of "haphazardness" applied to medieval
poor relief in general loses much of its point.

At first glance the canonistic doctrine seems simple enough.
The general responsibility of the bishop for feeding and protecting
the poor of his diocese was insisted on over and over again in
the *Decretum*. Here, for instance, are the comments of Gratian
himself introducing sections of the *Decretum* dealing with this
question: "In general the bishop shall provide necessities for
the poor and those who cannot work with their hands." "Bishops
ought to assist widows and orphans seeking the help of the
Church." "It behooves a bishop to be solicitous and vigilant
concerning the defense of the poor and the relief of the oppressed."
"Hospitality is so necessary in bishops that if any are found lacking
in it the law forbids them to be ordained." [1]

The word "hospitality" is of some importance because the phrase
most commonly used by the medieval canonists to describe the
poor relief responsibilities of the parish clergy was *tenere hospitalitatem*—they were obliged, that is, to "keep hospitality." The
primary sense of the word referred to the reception of travelers,
the welcoming of guests, but the canonists very often used it in
a broader sense to include almsgiving and poor relief in general.
This can be best illustrated from their comments on some of
Gratian's dicta. Thus, the words that Gratian used to introduce
St. John Chrysostom's much debated text on indiscriminate charity
were, "In *hospitality* there is to be no regard for persons," but
the canonists commonly took these words as a peg on which to
hang their disquisitions on the theory of almsgiving in general.
Again, when Gratian observed that a bishop should provide
necessities for the poor, the Ordinary Gloss commented that he

was treating the subject of "hospitality."[2] And at *Distinctio* 86, where Gratian introduced an elaborate discussion on episcopal poor relief responsibilities, several canonists explained that the whole section could be regarded as an extension of an earlier discussion on the virtue of hospitality.[3]

It is perhaps worth insisting at this point, since the fact has been denied by some scholars, that the poor who were to be provided for by the bishop of the diocese according to the decretist texts were the ordinary indigent lay folk and clergy, "the poor" in our normal everyday sense of the words. A different meaning is found in the pseudo-Isidorian decretals, a ninth-century collection of canons in which the phrase *pauperes Christi,* the poor of Christ, was used to describe monks who had chosen a life of voluntary poverty and who, accordingly, were regarded as worthy recipients of ecclesiastical charity. Some of the decretals in this collection were in fact forgeries, but they were universally accepted as genuine until the sixteenth century and many of them were included in the *Decretum.* G. G. Coulton maintained that the terminology of the forgeries introduced a radical distortion into the subsequent canon law of poor relief because, he held, Gratian's work "was practically founded on the pseudo-Isidorian collection" which "proved decisive in the matter of charity." Coulton added: "Thus the forgeries were in fact epoch making; and on no point more clearly, perhaps, than in the meaning they gave to the phrase 'Christ's Poor.' "[4] These views are quite mistaken. The overwhelming majority of Gratian's texts on poor relief were not derived from ninth-century forgeries but from genuine patristic material, especially from St. Ambrose and St. Augustine. Nor was the patristic material misinterpreted through the influence of forged texts. In *Distinctio* 86, which presents the core of the *Decretum*'s teaching on poor relief, there is really no ambiguity either in the texts themselves, or in Gratian's introductory remarks on them, or in the comments of the *Glossa Ordinaria.*[5]

In the texts of the *Decretum* the bishop was charged not only with a general duty of supervising the care of the poor, but also with a specific responsibility for dividing up the total revenue of the diocese in such a fashion that a due portion was distributed to those in need. "The bishop shall have the power of dispensing the property of the churches to the needy," declared the Council of Antioch as quoted by Gratian.[6] The classical division of ecclesiastical revenue was into four parts. The bishop was to retain one part for himself, distribute one part among his clergy, assign one part for the building and repair of churches, and use one part for the relief of the poor. This form of division was described in several texts of the *Decretum* dating back to the fifth century.[7] The phrase commonly used to describe the income to be so divided was *reditus et oblationes*, the "revenues and offerings" of the church. Later on, when the tithe was generally adopted as a form of compulsory ecclesiastical taxation, the same system of division was applied to it, though sometimes a threefold division was laid down: One part for the clergy, one part for church buildings, and one part for the poor. (This was the division prescribed for England in a law of King Ethelred in 1014.) But it does not seem to be true, as is often asserted, that in canonical theory the tithe came to be regarded as especially responsible for providing poor relief funds; the obligation of providing for the poor was attached to ecclesiastical income in general, not to the tithe in particular.

The only trouble about this simple and straightforward theory of poor relief, in which the bishop cares for all the poor of the diocese and assigns a specific proportion of the diocesan revenues for their support, is that it is utterly remote from the actual facts of diocesan organization in the high Middle Ages. Most of Gratian's texts on poor relief came from sources of the fourth to sixth centuries. In the intervening half-millennium before the *Decretum* was compiled a system had become established of dividing each diocese into parishes, with each parish a separate economic unit, and the parish priest directly responsible for administering the revenues accruing to his own church. These revenues came from three main sources: income from the land with which the church was endowed; the oblations or offerings of the people (in theory voluntary but in practice often fixed by custom for occasions like baptisms, marriages, funerals); and, most important, the tithe, which was a tax of 10 per cent on the produce of each parishioner. If the revenues of the church were to be used for the support of the poor these sources would have to contribute; but there could no longer be a simple division by the bishop as laid down by the early texts cited in the *Decretum* because such revenues did not come into the hands of the bishop to be divided.[8]

The situation was rendered much more complicated by a system of patronage that had grown up during the Dark Ages, when nearly all ecclesiastical revenues and ecclesiastical appointments fell under the control of the local feudal lords, so that the lord of a village regarded the revenues of the parish church as a mere private perquisite. The church reformers of the eleventh century bitterly attacked the whole principle of lay control over the Church, and, under their influence, many lay lords transferred their rights in parish churches to ecclesiastical institutions, very often to monasteries. The system that had emerged by the end of the twelfth century was a compromise between the demands of the reformers and the traditional rights of the lords. The patron of a parish might be a lay lord, perhaps the king himself, or it might be a monastery or some other ecclesiastical institution. The patron had the right of nominating the parson of the parish who would receive its revenues, but the nominee had to be approved by the local bishop who formally installed him in his church.

The importance of all this from our point of view is that the system made possible a diversion of parochial funds which could have been used for poor relief to absentee parsons who might know little and care less about the state and needs of their parishioners. This could happen in different ways. When an ecclesiastical institution, a monastery, say, was patron of a parish it might designate itself as a kind of corporate parson, and legally draw all the revenues of the church. The monastery would have to pay a priest to reside in the parish and say Mass for the people, but his wages would probably be only a fraction of the total revenue that the monks received from the parish. In those circumstances, the parish was said to be "appropriated" to the monastery. By the end of the twelfth century it was clearly established that any new appropriation required the consent of the bishop of the diocese, but such consent was in fact frequently granted, and appropriations of parish revenues to monasteries continued all through the Middle Ages.[9]

When a layman was patron of a parish he could not simply appropriate the church revenues for himself—not legally at any rate[10]—but he could appoint as parson a cleric who was a relative or perhaps a useful servant, and, again, the nominal parson might draw the revenues of the parish without residing there and pay some poor priest to do the actual work of the parish. The administrative departments of the royal government, especially the chancery in England, were staffed largely by clerics, and the king commonly provided for their salaries by presenting them to ecclesiastical benefices that lay in the royal patronage. On an ever-increasing scale, too, the popes, from the thirteenth century onward, began to exercise ecclesiastical patronage all over Christendom, and to provide in this way for their own growing armies of administrators. Sometimes, too, the income of a parish was used as a kind of scholarship fund to maintain a deserving scholar in one of the universities. The famous reformer, John Wyclif, lived much of his life at Oxford, drawing the income of two churches in widely separated parts of England, and hardly ever setting foot in either of them.

This diversion of parochial revenues, although open to serious abuses, was not in itself always intrinsically wicked. The income of the parishes varied enormously. The wealthiest of them had revenue enough to maintain a parson in luxury and feed the poor of the parish several times over. It was naturally the wealthier parishes that tended to be appropriated or assigned to absentees in the service of the patron, but it was not unreasonable that revenues greatly exceeding local requirements should be made available to serve the broader purposes of the Church. Even the appropriation of churches to monasteries, which became a particularly harmful abuse, had seemed justified in earlier days when the abbeys were the principal focal points of Christian culture and piety, and parish revenues that did not go to them were commonly seized and squandered by the local lord of the place. Again, most of the absentee rectors were not mere idlers but were employed in work of value to Christian society as a whole in the universities or in royal administration or in the service of the pope, work that had to be done by someone and had to be paid for somehow. The great danger inherent in the whole system was that it encouraged such absentees to regard the parish revenues they received as a private salary for work done away from the parish rather than as a public trust with corresponding obligations.

In view of this whole complex of circumstances it is obvious that the precise system of poor relief described in the old texts of the *Decretum* was not applied and could not have been applied in the conditions of the twelfth and thirteenth centuries, at least in regard to administrative detail. Hence it has commonly been assumed that in the high Middle Ages there was no effective system at all for regulating ecclesiastical revenues so that a due portion of them was applied to the relief of poverty. According to Ashley, "The old rules as to the employment of tithes, even as soon as the twelfth century, were in many places . . . not only little regarded but well-nigh forgotten." Coulton, on the other hand, maintained that everyone in the Middle Ages knew perfectly well that the poor were legally entitled to a third or at least a fourth of all tithes, but that the perverse ingenuity of the canon lawyers and the general wickedness of medieval ecclesiastics made it impossible for the poor to claim their rights in practice. The Webbs were equally pessimistic: "Already by the twelfth century, it seems, the tithe had ceased to supply any appreciable sum towards the relief of the poor . . . and, in spite of repeated injunctions, and even statutory provisions, it seems clear that, by the end of the fifteenth century at any rate, these absentee proprietors made no regular subventions for the poor of the parishes whence their revenues were derived." [11]

The implication here seems to be that if things were bad at the beginning of the twelfth century and worse at the end of the fifteenth, there could evidently have been nothing but deepening darkness in between. Yet the period of the high Middle Ages, say from mid-twelfth century to mid-fourteenth, saw one of the greatest flowerings of the human intellect and spirit which the world has known. It deserves to be judged as a civilization in its own right. Much of the best and most scholarly writing on the history of charity presents a false perspective by taking the whole period from the fall of the Roman Empire to the Renaissance as a single chronological unit for purposes of analysis. Hence Catholic apologists are prone to assume that the theories and practices of the patristic age remained unchanged until the Reformation, whereas critics of the medieval Church read back all the abuses of the later Middle Ages into the thirteenth century.

Ashley's assertion that the old law of the Church was well-nigh forgotten, and Coulton's assertion that the poor were still legally entitled to at least a fourth part of all tithes in the thirteenth century, are both deceptive oversimplifications. It would be by no means impossible a priori that the old law of the Church about the right use of ecclesiastical revenues was "well-nigh forgotten" at the beginning of the twelfth century and thoroughly well remembered at the end of it. There had, after all, been a great renaissance of legal studies in the meantime. As for the quadri-partite division of tithes, I am not sure that the early legislation which commanded the division of ecclesiastical revenues into four parts always did intend to insist rigorously on four equal parts. When one considers that the needs of the poor and the expenses connected with church building must have varied greatly from year to year, and that the sum needed for the upkeep of the clergy must have varied a great deal according to the number of priests in particular dioceses, such a system seems administratively im-practicable. But some of the popes who recommended it were very great practical administrators. Their intention was probably to define the various purposes for which church revenues could properly be used rather than to specify the precise arithmetical proportion to be spent on each. Certainly that is how their texts were taken by the canonistic commentators of a later age.[12] When, therefore, it is shown that nothing like 25 per cent or 33⅓ per cent of the total ecclesiastical income was devoted to the relief of poverty in medieval England, there is no need to assume that fundamental principles of canon law were being unscrupulously flouted. A quarter or a third of all church revenues would probably have amounted to a fantastic overprovision for the poor; and to condemn the medieval Church because of its failure to comply with the letter of the old law is about equivalent to condemning the population of modern Massachusetts for failing to observe literally the laws of the pilgrim fathers.

But, although the ancient legislation was no longer applicable in precise detail, its texts, embodied in the *Decretum,* continued to be studied by medieval canonists as exemplifying the basic principles concerning the obligation of the Church toward the poor. The real problem is to determine whether they succeeded in incorporating those principles into a code of law that really could have worked in the circumstances of their own age. We need to know what the current law prescribed before we can begin to consider how effectively it worked.

If any effective system of poor relief was to be based on the old texts there obviously had to be a good deal of adaptation, and there seem to be three essential requirements that had to be fulfilled if the adaptation was to be successful. First, the division of diocesan resources into parochial benefices had to be justified. Then it had to be made clear that the duty of providing funds for poor relief, attributed to the bishop in the old law, now devolved on the parsons of parishes, who were sharing in the revenues of the diocese. Finally, and most important of all, there had to be some provision to ensure that such responsibilities would actually be fulfilled, even when the parochial revenues were appropriated to an absentee rector.

The decretists treated the first point somewhat casually, though Gratian himself made rather heavy going of it. His main difficulty was that the assignment of specific endowments to an individual priest seemed to conflict with the rule that church property should be held in common. Moreover, one of his quotations from Pope Gelasius not only mentioned the customary fourfold division to be made by the bishop, but also explicitly forbade that any church endowments should be alienated permanently to the diocesan clergy. Gratian offered a rather rambling commentary on this which petered out in an acknowledgment that parochial benefices had in fact become established, without any real explanation of how the fact was to be reconciled with the authorities cited.[13] The *Summa Parisiensis* quite briskly dismissed the whole subject with the comment, "Gratian raises, on the side, a question about which today there is no doubt at all according to universal custom." Later on the author explained that the existence of individual benefices did not violate the rule about church property being held in common because the priest did not really own the property he administered, but could only take what he needed to support himself and was obliged to use the rest for the church and for the poor.[14] Joannes Teutonicus, in his *Glossa Ordinaria*, declared that the prohibition of Pope Gelasius applied only to the one particular diocese mentioned in the pope's letter, where the clergy were under suspicion of malpractices, and that, in general, church estates could quite properly be divided among individual priests. In fact Joannes thought that they were likely to be more efficiently managed under such an arrangement. He added that there were other texts of the *Decretum*, not quoted by Gratian in his argument, which conceded to the bishop authority to make such a division.[15]

As for the second stage of the adaptation, there was no doubt at all in the minds of the canonists that all holders of parochial benefices did acquire, along with their incomes, the financial responsibilities that the older laws attributed to the bishops, especially the responsibility toward the poor. William Lyndwood, in the fifteenth century, set this down in so many words: "The laws require that vicars and prelates be hospitable, . . . and although the laws mentioned speak specially of bishops, nevertheless you understand the same of other clerics." [16] In this he was merely restating the traditional point of view of the canonists. They were fond of quoting an observation of St. Jerome, incorporated in the *Decretum*, declaring that the clergy should be "content with food and clothes," [17] and also another saying of St. Jerome, likewise included in the *Decretum:* "Whatever the clergy has belongs to the poor. . . ." [18] Although such phrases became almost proverbial among the canonists, they are not to be taken quite literally. They must be understood in the light of the common teachings that the "food and clothes" necessary varied according to the "dignity, learning, and nobility" of the cleric concerned, and that a cleric had a right to draw an income from his benefice sufficient to maintain him in a style befitting his status, which might imply a very generous scale of living indeed.[19] But, while the canonists of the high Middle Ages insisted on the rights of a cleric in his benefice, they never forgot that the poor had rights in it too.

The point can be well illustrated from the *Glossa Ordinaria* to the Decretals of Pope Gregory IX where the issue arose in several different contexts. For instance, Bernardus Parmensis, commenting on a decretal forbidding priests to bequeath by will the property of their churches, said that the clergy had only the use of church property, not the ownership of it: "They ought to be content with food and clothes . . . and give all that is left to the poor." At another point in the Decretals it was laid down that the number of priests serving a church should be fixed according to the resources and expenses of the church. Commenting on this, Bernardus wrote that, in estimating the available resources, attention was to be paid to the expenses of hospitality which churches were bound to provide, as well as to the payments due to the bishop. Or, again, there is a decretal of Pope Innocent III rebuking a priest who had applied for an ecclesiastical appointment without revealing that he already possessed a sufficient benefice. This led Bernardus to raise the question: What constitutes a sufficient benefice? He replied that it was an amount sufficient to maintain the priest and his dependents fittingly, to pay the sums due to the bishop and to receive the needy who came for help.[20] Similar passages occur in other parts of Bernardus' gloss, and the same teaching is found in Joannes Andreae's *Glossa Ordinaria* to the *Liber Sextus*.[21]

Another group of texts clearly stating the obligation of an ecclesiastical benefice to provide funds for poor relief dealt with the canonical enforcement of charitable obligations. As noted previously, Joannes Teutonicus, at the beginning of the thirteenth century, taught that any rich man could be compelled by legal process to give alms to the poor. Later on this view became a subject of controversy, and it will be convenient to reserve an account of the controversy for a subsequent discussion. The point of immediate relevance is that, in considering this problem, the canonists sometimes made the point that there could be no doubt at all that a beneficed cleric was required to help the poor as a condition of holding his benefice, and could be compelled to do so by his ecclesiastical superiors if necessary. Zenzellinus de Cassanis provided a particularly detailed and interesting discussion of the point in his *Glossa Ordinaria* to the *Extravagantes Joannis XXII.* He distinguished between laity and clerics without benefices on the one hand, and beneficed clerics on the other. The first group, he thought, had a moral obligation but not a legally enforceable duty to show hospitality. But the clerics with benefices had a specific canonical obligation, enforceable by superiors, because "whatever the church has belongs to the poor." [22]

The canonists were rather vague in discussing the precise amount of hospitality that a church was required to provide. Joannes Teutonicus rather optimistically suggested that the proper income for a church would be enough to provide for everyone seeking help, but since the poor relief responsibilities of a parish were not limited to the parishioners themselves, it was hardly realistic to require that every church should be sufficiently endowed to meet all possible demands on it. Innocent IV pointed this out, declaring that each church should provide the amount of hospitality that was "due and customary," and Hostiensis and Zenzellinus de Cassanis wrote to the same effect.[23] This seems rather an evasion, but the canonists were laying down general principles of universal applicability in a situation where the actual needs varied greatly from place to place. Local churches could make their own more detailed regulations within the framework of established canonical principles. In England, for instance, a provincial council decreed in 1281 that hospitality was to be provided according to the resources of each church, "so that at least extreme necessity among poor parishioners is relieved." [24] (The decree, incidentally, provides a good example of how the word "hospitality" was used to include relief of the local poor as well as reception of travelers.) The canonists understood that the relief expenses of a parish church would vary greatly from place to place, that churches near a busy highway, for instance, would be especially subject to demands from beggars, and they thought such factors should be taken into account in considering what income was sufficient for a given place.[25]

Thus, although the canonists did not refer in precisely the same terms as the old laws to a priest's obligation to divide his income into so many parts, they did in fact require the parish revenues to be used for the purposes specified in the early texts. One part was to go to the priest himself, one part to the bishop (in the form of various taxes due from the parishes), one part to the poor. The canonists seem seldom to have mentioned the church fabric in these discussions, perhaps because responsibility for this varied according to local custom in different parts of Christendom. In England, for instance, the prevailing custom was that the parish parson was responsible for the upkeep of the chancel, the parishioners for the upkeep of the nave.

All this canonistic doctrine, however, would be quite meaningless if, in actual practice, the parochial revenue was alienated to some absentee parson who treated it as private income or to some remote monastery where the monks used it for their own purposes. The law relating to such alienations of parish revenues is therefore significant for the student of medieval poor relief, and it has a special interest since its study necessarily involves a comparison of the monastery and the parish as units of relief.

The issue arises at once from the terms of the appropriations themselves. In order to justify a new appropriation to the bishop who alone could authorize it, the monks had to show that they were in a state of "manifest poverty," that the resources of their monastery were insufficient to meet its necessary expenses. It became common form for the monks, when requesting a new appropriation, to assert that their house was overwhelmed by the burden of hospitality and that, without additional revenues, they could not meet this obligation. Their requests were often granted on this basis, so that, in effect, revenue that might have been used for poor relief in the parishes was siphoned off to monasteries to enable them to continue their charitable activities.

There has been much discussion as to whether the monasteries did in fact make a significant contribution to the relief of destitution, and, perhaps in reaction against the exaggerations of an earlier school of romantic medievalism, it has been the fashion lately to minimize their importance in this sphere. Nowadays, indeed, it is sometimes said that the final dissolution of the monasteries aggravated the problems of poverty in sixteenth-century England only by throwing a crowd of monastic servants and hangers-on onto the labor market, not by cutting off a major source of relief to the needy.

The most thoroughgoing investigation of monastic income and expenditure in England was made by A. Savine who worked on the *Valor Ecclesiasticus*, a survey of all the ecclesiastical incomes of England made in 1535 by order of Henry VIII for taxation purposes.[26] Certain specified charitable expenses were tax-exempt and these expenses were listed along with the gross incomes by the commissioners who compiled the *Valor*. From their figures Savine was able to show that the tax-exempt charitable expenditure of the monks amounted only to about 3 per cent of their total income. They were not allowed, however, to deduct all they spent on charity but only those sums that they were legally required to distribute by the terms of the original bequests. The figure of 3 per cent thus represents only that part of monastic revenues derived from property given to the monks to administer for some specified charitable purpose.

Another approach to this problem is to examine the surviving account rolls of individual abbeys, and here again the findings suggest that only a small percentage of the total monastic receipts was spent on the poor. R. H. Snape, in his book on English monastic finances, gave figures for half a dozen monasteries and concluded that, at the most optimistic estimate, only about 5 per cent of their revenues was spent on alms and hospitality.[27] Such figures are indeed significant, but caution is needed in interpreting them, for it is very difficult to extract really reliable information about charitable expenditures from medieval monastic accounts. In the first place, the sums set down as expenses of "hospitality" included money spent on the entertainment of wealthy visitors, which cannot reasonably be counted as charity. On the other hand, some genuine charitable expenses are very hard to estimate. For instance, the most common of all forms of monastic almsgiving was the distribution of leftover food from the monks' table to the poor. The elaborate care with which this distribution was regulated in itself suggests that the amounts involved must have been substantial and that food in excess of the monks' own requirements was commonly prepared in order to provide a surplus for the poor. But one can hardly hope to extract from medieval *compotus* rolls the kind of statistical information about such matters which is provided by modern techniques of cost accounting.

Again, the whole procedure of presenting the charitable expenditure of the monks as a percentage of their total receipts can be unhelpful and misleading if it is used as a basis for conclusions about the vitality of monastic life or the total effect of monastic alms. The accounts of a great modern business corporation would probably show that the amounts donated to higher education formed only a very small fraction of the corporation's total receipts. But it would be grossly misleading to conclude from this either that the corporation was a badly run business or that the total contributions of such corporations to higher education were negligible and could be suddenly cut off without seriously inconveniencing anybody. It was much the same with the monks. A monastery, after all, was not primarily an eleemosynary institution. The first business of the monks was to carry on from day to day the routine of corporate liturgical worship laid down in their rule. According to medieval ideas, the men who dedicated their lives to this supremely worthy task ought themselves to be supported in a decent and dignified fashion; it was also considered fitting that the worship of God should be carried on in magnificent buildings, and that incense, rich cloths, and precious metals should be used in religious ritual. The monks naturally, and properly, employed the bulk of their revenues for such purposes. But the visitation records of the high Middle Ages do not suggest that niggardliness in almsgiving was a very common complaint against the wealthier abbeys; the most detailed of all the episcopal registers that have come down to us from the thirteenth century, that of Archbishop Odo of Rouen, provides positive evidence of abundant monastic charity.[28] There seems no reason to doubt that conditions were similar in England or that, even on the eve of the Reformation, the monks were still providing a substantial contribution to the relief of destitution.

There is, however, another side to the question. The low percentage of monastic income devoted to charity does not necessarily indicate either that the monks were negligent or that their total contributions were negligible, but it does indicate that increasing the endowment of a monastery was not normally an efficient way of helping the poor. And if parishes could be stripped of all their funds on the pretext that monastic houses needed additional income to maintain hospitality, that was a real abuse. Monastic charity was likely to be more indiscriminate and less effective than alms administered by priests on the parochial level, and, even if the appropriating monasteries (or other absentee parsons) did give generously to the poor around them, there would still have been no provision for the destitute of the parishes that actually provided the funds.

This last point can be well illustrated from a dispute between the Bishop of Meath and the canons of Llanthony Priory in the year 1233, when both points of view were put forward with exceptional clarity. The bishop disputed the right of the canons to the revenues of certain parishes in his diocese and, in presenting his case, complained that "contrary to justice they cause to be carried away to their monastery of Llanthony near Gloucester the fruits and obventions of certain benefices that they have acquired in the diocese of Meath, which, by the common law [of the Church], ought to be distributed in the diocese of Meath to poor parishioners and others seeking hospitality. . . ." The canons replied to this argument that the parish revenues had been conferred on them in such a fashion that "their fruits and obventions might be expended for the sustenance of the brothers and of others resorting to their house at Llanthony, and not precisely in the diocese of Meath." They added that "they were not compelled by any law to distribute the goods of their churches in Meath, but that they could licitly turn them to the use of their monastery of Llanthony, to the increase of their hospitality and the sustenance of the brothers. . . ." [29]

It is interesting to find the issue debated in these terms in 1233. Just a year later, in 1234, the Gregorian Decretals were promulgated, and once they had been assimilated by the canonists, a monastery could hardly have claimed, as a matter of law, that it had no responsibilities toward the poor of the parishes that provided it with revenue. The lawyers and lawgivers of the medieval Church were quite alert to the problems that arose from abuse of patronage and appropriations and, from the late twelfth century onward, popes and councils were much concerned to ensure that the priest actually resident in a parish, whether it was the parson himself or a paid substitute, should have sufficient income to live decently and meet his various obligations, including that of caring for the poor.

Some abuses of patronage were dealt with in the Third Lateran Council, summoned by the great lawyer-pope, Alexander III, in 1179. This council decreed that no further appropriations were to take place without the consent of the local bishop, and that priests appointed to serve parishes held by monasteries were to be presented to the bishop for his approval.[30] If any patron who had the right and duty of appointing a parson to a parish failed to make an appointment after the parish had been vacant for three months, the bishop was to step in and make an appointment himself.[31] The final answer to the problem of appropriated parishes and absentee parsons in general was the institution of perpetual vicars. As long as a monastery or absentee parson could legally draw all the revenues of a parish and appoint to live there a hired priest, who was paid the minimum possible wage and was dismissable at will, there was little hope that the parishes would be adequately served. The popes and canonists therefore developed the doctrine that in every parish with a permanently absent parson there should be appointed a resident vicar, irremovable except by formal judicial process, and endowed with a fixed and adequate portion of the revenues of the church—the amount to be fixed by the bishop. This was finally promulgated as a universal law of the Church by the Fourth Lateran Council of 1215, the greatest representative assembly of medieval Christendom, in a canon that has been described as "the Magna Carta of the parish priest."[32]

This canon first called attention to the abuses that existed. In some places, the pope had heard, parish priests were receiving only one fourth of a fourth, or one sixteenth, of the tithes of the parish. Henceforth they were to be assigned a sufficient portion of the parish revenues. Whenever possible parsons were to reside in their parishes, but, if they did not do so, a perpetual vicar was to be appointed with, it was repeated, a suitable income assigned to him.

It has been complained that the pope required priests to have sufficient income without, however, explaining what a sufficient income was. But these are legal documents and it is easy enough to discover the meaning of their terminology by consulting the legal commentaries on them. The *Glossa Ordinaria* commented that the word *sufficiens* meant sufficient for the priest to live decently according to his "quality," to support any dependents, and to receive those who sought hospitality.[33] In any event there was an earlier letter of Pope Alexander III which became as important in the development of canonical doctrine as the decree of the Fourth Lateran Council itself, and which did explicitly mention that to "keep hospitality" was one of a vicar's duties and that he was entitled to an income sufficient for that purpose. Since this letter was written in reply to a query of the Bishop of Winchester on the point, at first it had only local significance, but it became a law binding on the whole Church when it was incorporated in the Gregorian Decretals of 1234, and was frequently cited by later canonists as the authoritative ruling on the point. In his letter Pope Alexander referred to monks who so burdened the vicars of their churches that they were unable to keep hospitality, and decreed that bishops were to refuse to accept vicars who were not endowed with sufficient income to meet their parish obligations and live decently.[34] The law was strengthened by a decretal included in the *Liber Sextus,* which laid down that a bishop could refuse to accept inadequately endowed vicars even when the monastery involved was one normally exempt from episcopal control.[35]

There still remained one difficulty. The law said clearly enough that the bishop should not accept a vicar appointed without sufficient income, but it did not explain what he should do if the monastery refused to make a suitable allotment. It would seem that there could be a deadlock, the monastery refusing to present an adequately endowed vicar, the bishop refusing to accept a vicar on the monks' terms. The issue was finally settled in 1311 by another general council, the Council of Vienne, which decreed that, in the circumstances described, the bishop should appoint the vicar presented by the monastery and himself assign to the vicar a suitable proportion of the parish revenues.[36] The canon of 1311 also explained that there could be an exception to the general rules regarding a vicar's income if the monastery undertook to meet all the expenses of the parish, and the *Glossa Ordinaria* explained that these would include the expenses of poor relief, of hospitality. The canonists thus recognized two legitimate arrangements. Either the appropriating body could itself assume responsibility for the obligations of the appropriated benefice, or else it was to appoint a vicar with sufficient income at his disposal to meet the expenses of the parish, including the burden of hospitality.

On the whole it seems that thirteenth-century legislators and lawyers were quite sensitive to the needs of the times and that, instead of merely repeating out-of-date platitudes, they developed a law of parochial incomes and parochial responsibilities which was well adapted to the circumstances of the age. How this law actually worked in practice is another question which will be considered in a separate chapter.

In addition to the parish and the monastery, the third great source of institutional charity in the Middle Ages was the hospital. The subject will be dealt with here more briefly than its intrinsic importance warrants, because it is the one topic in the whole field of medieval poor law which has been dealt with adequately in an excellent modern monograph, that of Jean Imbert.[37]

The twelfth and thirteenth centuries saw the foundation of very many hospitals by many different kinds of benefactors. Kings, bishops, feudal lords, wealthy merchants, guilds, and municipalities all endowed houses of charity. The hospitals themselves varied in purpose and in the way they functioned. There were leper colonies, orphanages, lying-in hospitals for pregnant women, homes for the aged and invalid. The smaller foundations tended

to specialize in some particular work of mercy, whereas great
institutions in the larger cities sometimes undertook a whole range
of charitable tasks. Some of the hospitals used all their funds for
their own inmates, some gave food to the same group of poor
each day who were fed by the hospital though not housed in
it, some gave to casual beggars. The word "hospital" is indeed
somewhat misleading. Medieval hospitals were not only institutions
providing medical care for the sick, but what we might call almshouses or settlement houses, homes for the aged and destitute
and centers of charitable activity. By the middle of the fourteenth
century there were more than 600 such institutions in England,
serving a population about as large as that of greater Los Angeles,
and ranging from numerous small houses caring for a dozen or
so inmates to great foundations like St. Peter's of York with its
permanent provision for the upkeep of 200 poor men.[38]

These institutions grew up with little detailed canonical regulation before the fourteenth century except for that provided
by the general principle that a bishop could intervene to prevent
maladministration of charitable bequests in his diocese. The
foundation of the hospital law of the later Middle Ages was the
decretal *Quia Contingit*, promulgated by Pope Clement V in 1311,
and subsequently incorporated in the *Extravagantes Joannis
XXII*.[39] This decretal called attention to various abuses which
had become notorious in hospital administration, and specifically
required bishops to inquire into the affairs of all hospitals in
their dioceses and to correct anything they found amiss. Moreover, all wardens of hospitals were to take a solemn oath to
administer with integrity the property entrusted to them, and, for
the future, they were to prepare an annual statement of the
accounts of their hospitals for the bishop. Most important of all,
this decretal laid down that, as a general rule, the wardenship
of a hospital was not to be regarded as an ecclesiastical benefice.
That meant not only that a layman could have charge of a hospital,
but also that its revenues could not be diverted from the purpose
intended by the founder to provide a handsome income for some
worthy or fortunate cleric. Its resources had to be devoted wholly
to the charitable purpose for which it existed except for any

reasonable stipend that might be assigned to the warden and his assistants.

The canonistic commentaries on hospital law are not so interesting for the student of poor law principles as might have been expected, and this is unfortunately true of the one medieval canonical treatise devoted exclusively to this subject, the *De Hospitalitate* of Lapi de Castelliono, written in mid-fourteenth century.[40] The church lawyers were much concerned with the detailed regulation of property rights and the definition of legal privileges, and in such matters their discussions have had a lasting influence on the law of charitable foundations down to the present day. But the canonists seldom discussed in detail the kind of administrative problems that have most perplexed writers on institutional poor relief in more recent times. There is very little, for instance, on criteria of admission to hospitals, or on the relative values of outdoor relief and institutional care in different types of cases. There was certainly no idea of a "workhouse test." The guests of a hospital were to be received and cared for in a spirit of Christian charity, though, as previously noted, the canonists did teach that the poor were not to be provided with sumptuous or lavish fare. This was sometimes urged on the moral ground that the poor ought not to be encouraged in luxurious tastes, sometimes on the common-sense ground that more poor people could be helped if the money available were not wasted on luxuries. But the main focal point of canonistic discussion on hospitals was the definition of their legal status as institutions in relation to the local parish and diocesan authorities, and on these matters Imbert's work should be consulted. Lapi de Castelliono, incidentally, justified the general supervisory authority of the bishop over hospitals on the ground that "to feed and care for the poor is a matter of public decency [*honestatis*]." [41]

In evaluating this whole pattern of canonistic thought and legislation it is above all important to bear in mind that, although the medieval Church did provide public poor relief, it was not only a poor relief agency nor primarily a poor relief agency. Like a modern government it had many other responsibilities besides that of providing public relief, and many other calls on its revenues.

The duty of the bishop was to ensure that the revenue of his diocese was expended in such a way as to promote the public welfare. Certainly, to any medieval man, it seemed conducive to the public welfare that prayers should be offered to God, and that communities of monks should be fittingly maintained to carry on the highest form of prayer. It seemed entirely legitimate therefore for bishops to divert surplus parochial funds to the upkeep of monasteries. Again, like a modern government, the Church needed administrators, judges, and diplomats who had to maintain staffs of clerks and had to mix in the highest circles of society. Such men needed large incomes if they were to do their work effectively, and, again, it was not necessarily an abuse if surplus parochial revenues were diverted to them.[42] The considerations that would influence a bishop in providing for the superior sort of clergy are reflected in a document of Anthony Bek, Bishop of Durham, dated 1286. The bishop divided the revenues of the wealthy parish of Chester-le-Street into several benefices to provide a comfortable endowment for a number of priests in a new collegiate church. He justified this by pointing out that the revenues available were sufficient to support several clerics to celebrate the divine office and provide more diligent cure of souls. "Moreover," he added, "there were lacking in the diocese lawyers and councillors to aid the bishop in the arduous affairs of his church." [43]

Again, an argument of Henricus de Bohic illustrates the kind of flexibility that was sometimes needed in protecting the interests of the poor while at the same time promoting the public welfare. Henricus asked whether it could ever be licit for a bishop to divert a charitable bequest for the poor to some other worthy purpose, like repairing the parish church. After giving a series of arguments against this, he pointed out that the bishop had an equal duty to feed the poor, maintain churches, and provide for the clergy. Moreover, it was in the interests of the poor themselves that churches should be maintained, since alms for the poor were collected in them. His conclusion was that, if the church was in such a bad state that the people could not assemble for worship, and if there were no other funds available for repairing it, and if the poor would not suffer any great harm from the diversion of the bequest, then the bishop might permit it to be used for the church. But if any of these conditions was not fulfilled he could not do so.[44] The bishop had to weigh all the relevant factors and do what was best for the public good, having regard to the needs of the poor.

By the thirteenth century the bishop no longer disposed directly of all the ecclesiastical revenues within his diocese, but he had broad powers of jurisdiction which gave him authority to check any abuses in the administration of those revenues. By exercising his rights of visitation and correction in parishes and monasteries, by supervising the conduct of privately endowed charities, by prudently weighing all the circumstances in granting or withholding permission for appropriations and absenteeism, a conscientious bishop could ensure that the revenues available were used for the ends prescribed by canon law. And the canon law clearly laid down that one responsibility that should not be neglected was the provision of poor relief.

CHAPTER

V   Theory and Practice

"Another constant claim [on parish priests] was the relief of the poor, strangers and wayfarers. . . . This claim, there can be no doubt, was fully accepted and carried out." [1] Abbot Gasquet wrote these cheerful words in 1906. Actually there has been a great deal of doubt. Ashley thought it "improbable that the ordinary parochial clergy distributed in alms any large part of their income," and he was convinced that Chaucer's "poor parson" could only have been portrayed as an exception to the general rule in that

Full loth were him to cursen for his tithes,
But rather wolde he yeven out of doute
Unto his poure parishens aboute
Of his offring and eke of his substance.[2]

E. M. Leonard, in the pages on medieval charity introducing her study of Tudor and Stuart poor law, scarcely mentioned any canonical provision for poor relief from parish funds.[3] And the Webbs thought that parochial relief was almost nonexistent in the high Middle Ages simply because all the available revenues had been diverted to other purposes.[4]

The writer who above all others devoted himself to attacking Gasquet's arguments was G. G. Coulton, and it is mainly owing to the effect of his trenchant criticisms that Gasquet's conclusions on this point have never found much acceptance.[5] The skirmishing over poor relief administration was only a minor engagement in an extensive warfare between these two regarding the whole state of the medieval Church and its impact on contemporary society. Gasquet knew much of the source material at first hand, but he was handicapped by an apparently congenital blindness to all the less edifying aspects of medieval Catholicism and by a somewhat cavalier attitude to the conventions of historical documentation. Coulton was equally biased in the other direction but usually much more scrupulous in citing the sources on which he based his arguments. When canonistic sources were in question, however, he was evidently on unfamiliar ground and he stumbled into some odd misinterpretations in expounding them. Both protagonists are dead now, and no sensible historian would wish to discuss the issues they debated in terms that might stir up any remaining animosities. But one can hardly traverse this ground without an occasional reference to the background of earlier controversy, and it would be unrealistic to sketch in the pattern of thirteenth-century legislation and legal theory without making any attempt to investigate its practical applications.

In considering the parish priests' ability to provide hospitality on a significant scale Gasquet certainly laid himself open to criticism by suggesting that the appropriation of parish revenues never did constitute a serious abuse in medieval England, and Coulton was certainly right to point out that the abuses were flagrant and numerous. But by concentrating on the abuses practically to the exclusion of all else he presented a picture as remote from reality as Gasquet's sunlit landscape of a medieval Merry England. After all, medievalists know that abuses can be detected in all medieval institutions if they are scrutinized closely enough, and poor law administrators know that abuses can be detected in all poor relief systems if they are scrutinized closely enough. So to prove that there were abuses in the medieval poor relief system really does not help very much. Any description of such abuses should provide only a background for an investigation of the normal prevailing practice, not a substitute for such investigation. Above all, it is quite possible to agree with Coulton that there were many abuses in the administration of parish revenues in the Middle Ages without feeling any compulsion to agree with Ashley and the Webbs that the total amount of parochial relief was negligible.

In seeking to establish how far, if at all, the canonical principles discussed in the last chapter were really applied in practice in thirteenth-century England, it is as well to begin with the question of the recipients of parish revenues. For, if no poor relief funds were available in the parishes, any further inquiry into the administration of the law relating to their expenditure would be futile. Gasquet indeed cited several instances where vicars of appropriated parishes enjoyed incomes of 10, 20, even 30 pounds a year, with the optimistic observation that such instances could be multiplied indefinitely.[6] Incomes of that size would certainly have permitted priests to contribute significantly to the relief of the poor of their parishes. But Coulton pointed to many more vicars who had stipends of only about 3 or 4 pounds a year, barely enough to support themselves, let alone help the poor. For our purpose neither Gasquet's half-dozen instances of very rich vicars nor Coulton's 200 or 300 instances of very poor vicars are particularly helpful. There were, after all, somewhat more than 8,000 parishes in medieval England. Moreover, most writers seem to have approached this problem by considering how much was taken out of the parishes, whereas the only really significant question for a student of poor relief is: How much was left in? By the end of the thirteenth century, perhaps a fourth of the parishes of England were appropriated, and some of these were served by scandalously underpaid vicars or by no vicar at all. If one is looking for abuses it is entirely legitimate to dwell on these facts. If one is simply trying to discover the normal state of affairs it is perhaps more relevant to remember that three-fourths of the parishes were not appropriated, and that among those that were a substantial number at any rate were served by comfortably endowed vicars as the law required.

One thing that does seem to be generally agreed among medieval historians is that the English bishops of the thirteenth century strove zealously to implement the decree of the Fourth Lateran Council concerning appointment of vicars, and, in general, worked to secure adequate incomes for the parish clergy.[7] The most recent investigation indeed suggests that the work was well under way even before the council of 1215 gave it an added stimulus.[8] How far the bishops were successful in their endeavors is a much more arguable question. There is some difficulty, in the first place, in deciding what was a reasonable income for a parish priest in thirteenth-century money. A figure of about 5 pounds a year has been suggested as enough to provide a decent standard of life for the priest himself and his immediate household, and that seems reasonable enough in view of the fact that most of the lower clergy came from the families of small yeoman farmers or artisans. A highly skilled craftsman—a first-rate carpenter or stonemason—earned about 4 pence a day in the thirteenth century, and that works out at around the same figure of 5 pounds in the year. An unskilled laborer might earn only half that and still have enough to keep body and soul together.[9]

The minimum stipend for vicars in England laid down in the provincial synod of Oxford in 1222 seems a little lower than this, for it was only 5 marks a year (a mark was 13 shillings and 4 pence, or two-thirds of a pound).[10] But the provision stipulated that the benefice should be one that could be "farmed" for 5 marks a year, that is, of such a value that an agent would pay 5 marks a year for the privilege of collecting and keeping the revenues. This was a very common way of assessing the value of an office in the Middle Ages. The asumption was, of course, that the agent would make a profit, so the actual value of a benefice that could be farmed for 5 marks was probably at least 5 pounds, and since, in practice, the vicar was required to reside in his parish and would collect his own revenues, the amount accruing to him would be 5 pounds.

It is a little startling to read in a decree of another English synod of the thirteenth century that, even on this income, a vicar was expected to provide hospitality. But the wording of the decree itself helps to explain the situation. It laid down that each vicar should receive at least 5 marks, "out of which he can keep hospitality according to the measure of his resources, and be sustained if he falls into sickness, old age or other disablement." [11] The implication seems to be that the vicar would naturally not rely solely on the 5 marks for his own support provided that he was hale and hearty. In fact, to say Mass and administer the sacraments in a poor rural parish of a few dozen families was not necessarily a full-time job, and the canon law explicitly provided that poor priests could augment their incomes by working at some honorable occupation.[12] The normal practice in an English village was for a vicar of yeoman stock to rent land and farm it. Coulton expended a great deal of sympathy on the poor vicar "starving on five marks a year"; but, in practice, a vicar with a benefice valued at 5 marks a year probably had about 5 pounds a year (a skilled craftsman's pay) plus a substantial house and garden plus whatever he chose to earn by his own efforts. Altogether he was very much better off than the majority of the villagers to whom he ministered.

Some vicars of this sort no doubt did what they could for the poor. In a letter dated 1291, Archbishop Romeyn of York commends such a one as "a poor cleric who, not sparing hospitality, receives those who come liberally, and cares for the poor according to the measure of his means." [13] But it is obvious enough that, although priests at this income level were far from "starving" themselves, they did not possess the resources to contribute substantially to the needs of others.

Thus far, however, we have been considering only minimum

incomes within the law, not average incomes, and the important thing to know is the average or median income for priests actually resident, doing the work of a parish, whether parsons or vicars. The best source for this information, though a very imperfect one, is the *Taxatio Nicholai IV*, an assessment of ecclesiastical incomes made in 1291 to serve as a basis for future taxation.[14] It is in some ways an exasperating piece of work. The commissioners who compiled it worked more carefully in some dioceses than in others. As a general rule, in each parish, the income of the parson is given and then the income of the vicar where there was a vicar. In such parishes it can be taken that the parson was an absentee, and that the actual income available for the work of the parish was the vicar's income. Where no vicarage is listed it can normally be assumed that the parson was actually resident, caring for the parish himself; but there would have been a sprinkling of parishes where the parson was temporarily absent with episcopal permission or had illegally deserted his benefice. Moreover, quite often a vicar's income was listed without a corresponding figure for the parson, and sometimes no vicarage was listed in a parish where we know from other sources that there actually was a vicar. But when all these things are taken into account, it still remains true that the *Taxatio* provides a great compendium of information about more than 8,000 English parochial benefices.

The most important factor to be taken into account in any critical use of this information is the fact that, in the thirteenth century as in the twentieth, income assessed for tax purposes was substantially lower than income actually received. It was established by Rose Graham that this principle holds good for the assessment of 1291, and subsequent research has tended to confirm her conclusions. Miss Graham cited instances when the assessed income was only half the real income of a benefice, and R. A. R. Hartridge added, "I doubt whether the figures often do represent more than half the true value." [15] That is my own impression too. The whole of the *Taxatio* was analyzed by E. L. Cutts in an old but very perceptive work on medieval English parishes. He found 8,085 churches listed, with 1,487 vicarages mentioned among them (but this is certainly an underestimate of the total number of appropriated churches).[16]

The only breakdown by income given by Cutts was a list of the total number of benefices assessed at less than ten marks a year; he found 2,711 parsons and 1,125 vicars in this class. Such figures are not very adequate for the purpose of this inquiry, especially since Cutts was convinced that the assessed incomes were equal to the actual revenues of the benefices. It would indeed be a formidable task to attempt a detailed statistical summary of all the figures in the *Taxatio*. It does seem worthwhile, however, to present a more elaborate breakdown than Cutts's for at least a significant sample, and for this purpose I have chosen the small diocese of Chichester. It is especially suitable for analysis, because an exceptionally large number of vicarages was listed for it. Even benefices too poor to be liable for taxation were scrupulously recorded for this diocese, and altogether the picture is unusually detailed. Moreover, it should not give an unduly favorable impression, for, according to Cutts's figures, the proportion of benefices under ten marks was rather higher in the diocese of Chichester than in the whole of England.

The figures given below represent, as far as they can be ascertained from the *Taxatio*, the assessed incomes of the priests actually charged with the work of parishes. That is to say, for a parish having a vicar, only the vicar's income is included, not the parson's. Also, a few parishes that were apparently appropriated, but for which no vicarages were mentioned, are excluded. So, too, are cathedral prebends, for it would perhaps be optimistic to suppose that canons of the cathedral always resided in the parishes that provided their incomes. The vicarages established in some of the prebends are, however, included. On this basis there remain 273 incomes for parsons and vicars. They break down like this:

	Above £25	£20–25	£15–20	£10–15	£8–10	£6–8	£5–6	£4–5	Below £4
Parsons	8	11	9	42	15	24	27	21	2
Vicars	—	—	2	15	13	23	37	23	1
Parsons and vicars	8	11	11	57	28	47	64	44	3
Percentage of total	3	4	4	21	10	17	23	16	1

In this sample 82 per cent of the parish priests had assessed incomes of £5 or more, 59 per cent of about £7 or more, and 32 per cent of £10 or more. But the actual incomes may have been nearly double these figures. If the assessed incomes are increased by 50 per cent so as to approximate the real incomes, and this is probably a conservative estimate, 59 per cent of the sample had incomes of about £10 or more, and 82 per cent had incomes of £7 10s. or more. The median income was a little more than £10. Investigations of other samples from the *Taxatio* have produced similar results, and although figures like this are only indicative, not definitive, they do indicate pretty clearly that the typical incumbent of a thirteenth-century English parish was not really a "starving vicar."

The figures also indicate, however, that in many parishes the priest's benefice did not in itself provide any substantial surplus that might have been applied to poor relief. But, in estimating the availability of parish relief funds, there are other factors to be considered. In the first place the income that a parson or vicar received from his ecclesiastical benefice was very commonly not his total income. Priests of peasant or yeoman stock supplemented their incomes by their own work, and priests of a higher social status often had means of their own. In the ten-year period, 1328–1337, 60 per cent of the ordinands in the diocese of Hereford claimed that they could support themselves from their own private resources.[17] In the second place, the total income of the parson or vicar does not represent the total sum from which poor relief could be supplied. The parishioners did not discharge all their financial obligations to the church by paying tithe. It is generally known, for instance, that they were required to contribute additional sums toward the upkeep of the church fabric. It is perhaps not so generally understood that medieval canon law required them also to contribute to the upkeep of the poor over and above what they paid in tithes. The doctrine laid down in the *Decretum* was that the parishioners should pay tithes in full and then give to the poor out of the nine parts that remained, and in the Decretals, parish priests were instructed to see that their parishioners did not neglect this duty.[18] The terms of Pope

Nicholas IV's bull commanding the tax assessment of 1291 imply that such contributions were commonly collected in thirteenth-century parishes. In this bull the pope specified at length the types of parochial revenue which were exempt from taxation, and in this class he included the sums collected "by clerics or laity" for various pious causes, including the care of the poor and the decent burial of dead paupers.[19] Again, as Ashley pointed out, a common form of medieval charity was to leave an endowment for the poor of a parish under the administration of the parish priest.

When these circumstances are taken into account, it seems that for a parish to have been utterly lacking in poor relief funds must have been very much the exception rather than the rule. There is one further point to be made. Much of the destitution arising in the ordinary course of village life from old age or sickness was alleviated in the Middle Ages by the customary land law, by family connections, or by voluntary societies. A major call on the parish funds must have been to provide additional assistance for folk who were already maintained at or near the barest subsistence level. In such circumstances the existence of even small funds in most of the parishes could have had a considerable effect in mitigating the total mass of human misery.

The canon law relating to parish relief cannot then be simply shrugged aside as inapplicable because of a universal lack of parish funds. But the question remains whether there was in fact any serious attempt to enforce the law. It may be that legislation was promulgated at Rome with pomp and ceremony, and quietly ignored in the provinces. That is often the way of things in far-flung empires, ecclesiastical as well as secular. And perhaps all the elaborate jurisprudence about church property and its obligations was mere "cobweb of the brain," spun out by academic lawyers in the universities and bearing no relation to real life.

One useful approach to this problem is to consider how far, if at all, the general legislation of the Church was repeated and developed in the decrees of local councils, for, in an age without printing and without the elaborate apparatus of communications through which subordinates are controlled in modern large-scale organizations, the diocesan synod was the principal channel through which the ordinary parish clergy could be informed of the ecclesiastical law to which they were supposed to conform. The bishop knew the canon law, or, at any rate, he had expert advisers who did, and, in local councils attended by the clergy of his diocese, he could call attention to abuses that existed and reënact as synodal statutes the provisions of canon law which were designed to check them. The essential functions of synodal legislation, then, were to publicize the rules of general law that the bishop particularly wished to enforce and, if necessary, to supplement them with administrative instructions adapted to local circumstances.

If there were no references to poor relief in this local legislation, it could indeed be assumed that the relevant canon law existed only in the books of the lawyers and was probably unknown to the priests who, in the last resort, had to carry out its provisions. But, in fact, the subject is dealt with in some of the most influential collections of English synodal statutes of the thirteenth and fourteenth centuries. Apart from frequent legislation concerning the appointment of adequately endowed vicarages, and protests against the diminution of hospitality through pluralities and absenteeism, there are a number of positive enactments concerning the care of the poor. They reveal, moreover, a significant development in ideas which reflects the general trend of canonistic thought during the period. At first there are only general commands that all the clergy, and monks in particular, ought to be generous and hospitable to the poor. Later on there is a clearer awareness that the parish as an institution had a specific responsibility to its poor parishioners, and that this responsibility had to be fulfilled even when the parish was appropriated to a monastery whose monks were themselves providing hospitality in their own district.

The first synodal statutes to be promulgated in England after the Lateran Council of 1215 were those of Richard Poore, Bishop of Salisbury from 1217 to 1228, and himself a doctor of canon law.[20] These statutes have been described as "by far the most efficient and exhaustive of the collections published during this period and . . . worthy to be a model to those who followed after";[21] and they did indeed serve as a model for several other bishops in the first half of the thirteenth century. In these statutes Bishop Poore decreed that "priests and beneficed clergy be hospitable according to their revenues and resources, and not miserly to the poor," and added that monks were especially bound to observe this rule.[22] The provincial Council of Oxford, summoned by Archbishop Stephen Langton in 1222, dealt with many matters of church discipline, and in the field of poor relief decreed "that prelates have honorable clerics as almoners and be hospitable . . . and that at suitable hours they appear in public to hear suits and do justice." [23] Another set of statutes, probably issued in the diocese of Coventry in the 1220's, likewise required priests to show hospitality.[24]

The next very influential set of synodal statutes was promulgated by Walter de Cantilupe, Bishop of Worcester, in 1240. It repeated Bishop Poore's injunction with some added detail: "We command that all clerics, and especially monks, shall exercise hospitality . . . according to the extent of their resources and without murmuring since, according to Scripture, a gentle word is better than a gift." The decree added that priests should be especially careful not to neglect those from whom they had nothing to hope or fear whether they received them or not.[25] Another statute of Bishop Cantilupe laid down that, when a parson was absent from his parish without episcopal permission, a quarter of his revenues were to be confiscated and spent on "the poor parishioners and other pious causes." [26] The statutes of Bishop Richard Wych of Chichester (1244–1253) repeated the usual instruction to parish priests: "We decree that [parsons] shall reside in their own churches, paying attention to hospitality and other works of charity according to their resources." But now we find added to this an explicit command that in appropriated churches vicars were to care for the poor and were to be sufficiently endowed to enable them to do so: "We wish also that in parish churches belonging to monks there be established vicars who are willing and able to watch over the safety of souls and to them we wish to be assigned a portion [of the revenues] out of which the ministers of the church may be suitably maintained, and the vicars may be able to show themselves hospitable to the poor, having regard to the resources of the church." [27] The obligation of vicars to provide hospitality was repeated in the statutes attributed to Giles of Bridport, Bishop of Salisbury (1257–1262), and in those of Peter Quivil, Bishop of Exeter (1280–1291).[28]

Another group of statutes dealt with the provision of poor relief for appropriated parishes or parishes with absentee parsons where, for some reason, there was no adequately endowed permanent vicar. John Gervais, Bishop of Winchester (1262–1265), decreed that all nonresident recipients of parish revenues were to spend on their poor parishioners a sum to be determined by the bishop, but to be not less than a tenth of the tithes.[29] This decree was very likely inspired by a letter that Pope Alexander IV sent to a group of English bishops in 1261, in which the pope took note of abuses arising from appropriations and laid down that one-eighth or one-tenth of the revenue of appropriated churches was to be allotted to the poor of the parish concerned.[30] The decree of Bishop Gervais and the pope's letter both added that this rule did not have to be enforced when the appropriated parish was in the immediate vicinity of the monastery; presumably the parishioners would then share in the normal monastic almsgiving.

In 1281 John Peckham, Archbishop of Canterbury, summoned another provincial council, the Council of Lambeth, which legislated for all the dioceses of the province of Canterbury. Its statutes again included a decree *On Keeping Hospitality:* "We decree that rectors of churches who do not reside in their churches nor have vicars should exercise the grace of hospitality through their agents, according as the resources of their churches suffice and so that at least the extreme need of the poor parishioners is relieved. . . ." [31] (Two years later we find Bishop Peter Quivil of Exeter granting a license for nonresidence with the added words, "saving the canonical portion to be assigned by the bishop to the poor of the parish as was decreed in the last Council of Lambeth." [32]) Archbishop Stratford enacted a similar statute in his provincial council of 1342. He complained that monasteries with appropriated parishes were neglecting their duty toward the parishioners, and continued: "Wherefore, with the approval of this sacred council, we decree that the above-mentioned religious holding appropriated ecclesiastical benefices shall be compelled by the bishops to distribute each year to the poor parishioners of those benefices a certain quantity of alms to be assessed by the local bishops according to the resources of the benefices, under pain of sequestration of the fruits and revenues of the benefices. . . ."[33]

Finally, in this connection, a pronouncement of one of the greatest English bishops of the thirteenth century seems relevant, although it is not a synodal statute. In 1250 Bishop Grosseteste of Lincoln delivered an address before the papal curia on the evils of appropriations and absentee rectors, and in the course of it used these words: "Moreover, the work of pastoral care consists not only in the administration of Sacraments and the saying of canonical hours, and the celebration of masses. . . . It consists in the feeding of the hungry, in giving drink to the thirsty, in clothing the naked, in receiving guests, in visitation of the sick and prisoners, especially of one's own parishioners, to whom the temporal goods of the churches belong."[34] These are not the words of an academic lawyer but of a great administrator who for nearly twenty years had been governing the largest diocese in England with conspicuous vigor, and who had been especially active in the visitation of his churches and in the endowment of vicarages. It is hard to believe that any comfortably endowed parish priest in Grosseteste's diocese was allowed to forget his canonical obligation to relieve the poor.

Local synods and episcopal pronouncements seem closer to real life than the theories of academic lawyers, but they are still in the realm of legislation and exhortation rather than of actual administrative enforcement. The obvious place to turn for information on this last subject would seem to be the administrative records of the bishops, the episcopal registers, but in fact they do not provide very abundant evidence. A large number of English bishops' registers survives from the thirteenth century, but they vary greatly in content, and none of them provides anything like a complete account of all the administrative acts of any one bishop. A good example of their limitations as source material is provided by the register of St. Thomas de Cantilupe, Bishop of Hereford. He was a man renowned for his good works and bountiful charity.

After his death a great popular devotion grew up around his burial place, and in 1320 he was formally canonized. But on the basis of his episcopal register alone he might be judged simply an avaricious and litigious prelate, for the register consists in large part of elaborately detailed records concerning the various lawsuits in which he was engaged throughout his episcopate. The truth is, of course, that it was part of his duty as a bishop to defend the property of his church, by lawsuits if necessary, and that he thought it more important to preserve a record of these legal proceedings than of his other activities. In the same way each bishop set down in his register only those matters of which he most wanted a permanent record—and often they are not the matters of most interest to modern scholars.

There is then no negative "argument from silence" in interpreting the registers. But they can be helpful insofar as they provide any scraps of positive evidence regarding the enforcement of the canon law on poor relief. By far the most interesting from this point of view is the register of Archbishop Peckham, who not only promulgated legislation on the care of the poor but evidently insisted on its being obeyed. In 1282 he rebuked Bogo de Clare, a notorious pluralist, in these terms: ". . . you have not fulfilled the office of a rector but rather of a ravisher because, while gathering the goods of the poor, you minister little or nothing to them." [35] Two years later there came a season of great scarcity, and the archbishop wrote to his *officialis* instructing that the law of parochial poor relief was to be strictly enforced. It was clear from both the Old and New Testaments, he wrote, that a Christian pastor was bound to provide for his flock in both spiritual and temporal things. Accordingly, "you are to compel by your letters all rectors and vicars of our jurisdiction to provide for their subjects according to the adequacy of their resources in this time of pernicious famine, as the laws of the Gospel and the canon laws subordinate to them plainly lay down." [36]

That was in February, 1284. Three months later the archbishop himself came upon a case of flagrant neglect and took prompt action. In passing through the parishes of Wrotham and Lyming, both held by an absentee parson, one Peter Blaunc, he found the cure of souls neglected and "the poor parishioners afflicted with hunger through lack of a good provider." Peckham wrote a stinging letter to Peter Blaunc informing him that he had discovered this state of affairs, requiring him to dispense alms to the value of five pounds at once in each of his parishes, and summoning him to a meeting to discuss the future administration of his churches. In October the Queen of France, no less, wrote to request that her clerk Peter Blaunc be made available to assist her in important business. The archbishop replied that he could not accede to the request "at least until he [Blaunc] shall provide in some fashion for the souls committed to his care." [87]

Then, in 1287, Peckham promulgated a set of eight articles that were to be kept in writing in each parish church and to be read out from time to time "so that they may frequently occur to the memory of the ministers." The third of these articles reminded the clergy that they should "provide for the bodily necessities of the poor and needy, especially for those of their cure, according as the resources of the church suffice." [88]

The episcopal registers provide abundant evidence concerning the establishment of vicarages in appropriated churches, but in the documents defining the vicars' rights and responsibilities there is seldom any explicit reference to poor relief. This is not particularly significant, however, because the vicarage ordinations usually did lay down that the vicar was to sustain "all the due and customary burdens" (*omnia onera debita et consueta*) of the church. All parties must have been well aware that to "maintain hospitality" was canonically one of the *onera debita*. In one well-known case, the appropriation of the church at Lindridge to the priory of Worcester in 1307, the rights of the poor were explicitly defended by the bishop against the king himself. The appropriation was requested on behalf of the priory by King Edward I, but even so Bishop Swinfield of Hereford at first refused to sanction it, an act of some courage for Edward was one of the most formidable of medieval English monarchs. When the king reiterated his demand with considerable show of irritation the bishop gave way, but only on terms of his own making. It was feared, he wrote, that the priory would neither keep hospitality nor distribute the usual alms in the parish; he agreed, however, that the appropriation should take place on the death of the parson then in possession, but only on condition that a suitable and sufficient portion of the revenues would be reserved for a vicar, "from which he can keep hospitality and distribute alms to the poor parishioners in the customary fashion." Three years later the appropriation took place and the vicar was assigned a quite handsome income of twenty marks.[39] Sometimes, no doubt, the appropriating institutions were more scrupulous than Bishop Swinfield expected the priory of Worcester to be. The financial records of the dean and chapter of Lincoln suggest that some regard was paid to the welfare of poor parishioners in their appropriated churches.[40]

One point on which there is frequently evidence that the law was enforced is the requirement that parsons absent from their parishes should make some provision for the poor. Most of the examples occur in parishes where the parson had obtained a license of nonresidence for a specified period to study at a university. These licenses often included a provision that a specified sum was to be paid to the poor of the parish during the period of absence.[41] It must be added that there were many more licenses without this specific provision, but even they commonly included a general condition that the parish should not be defrauded of any due services. The meaning of the phrase "due services" was explained by Archbishop Peckham. He wrote that he himself had granted licenses of nonresidence to certain priests, but that he had always intended that their churches should by no means be defrauded of any due service; and, he added, "We know to be among the foremost of such services those by which not only the spiritual life but the corporal life of their subjects is provided for." [42]

The most satisfactory evidence of law enforcement or neglect of it would come from detailed accounts of the actual findings in parochial visitations, but here the evidence is very scanty indeed for the thirteenth century. The visitation records of the churches belonging to St. Paul's Cathedral contain almost no information about the conduct of the vicars, but are for the most part mere inventories of the possessions and revenues of the churches, with

notes on dilapidations of church buildings.[43] The published episcopal registers of the period contain references to visitations but
no detailed accounts of the findings, though occasionally there
are indications that almsgiving was among the topics to be in-
quired into. When Archbishop Winchelsey set out to visit the
dioceses of his province he proposed to ask each bishop whether
he was accessible to the complaints of the poor, and "whether he
was hospitable, merciful, and gave alms, and whether he had an
honorable cleric as almoner." Cathedral canons were to be asked
whether they kept hospitality as was proper and gave alms to
the poor.[44] Bishop Bronscombe of Exeter required his archdeacons
to make strict inquiry as to whether parish priests were using
their revenues for the purposes specified in canon law or were
wasting them in luxuries. They were to indict offenders before
the bishop's *officialis*.[45] Another set of thirteenth-century visitation
articles, which may have been used by Archbishop Boniface of
Canterbury in 1253, contained the question "whether any layman,
or anyone of whatsoever condition or reputation has perished,
the rector or vicar of the place being aware of it." [46]

For the early part of the fourteenth century there is a little more
evidence, especially for the diocese of Exeter. In 1328 Bishop
John de Grandisson inspected the chapter of his cathedral church,
and recorded as an abuse to be remedied that some of the canons
had failed in their duty to the poor.[47] The register of Bishop
Walter de Stapledon (1307–1326) is unusually informative about
parochial visitations. The procedure on these occasions was for
a group of parishioners, usually four, to give evidence on oath
regarding the state of the parish and the conduct of the priest,
and Bishop Stapledon's register contains many such depositions.
It is encouraging to note that the parishioners usually reported
that their priest was a decent and honorable character, and their
frequent mention of some little peccadillo to which they took
exception serves only to give an air of reality to their evidence.
The vicar of Culmstock, for instance, was described as a man of
good life and honorable conduct: "They knew of nothing reprehensible in him as to the visiting of the sick, the baptizing of
infants, and all other things that pertained to his office except this,

that—as it seemed to them—he delayed too long between Matins and Mass on feast days." [48]

Sometimes, of course, there were more serious accusations, but there is hardly ever a complaint that the priest refused to give alms. The only instance in the register concerns the collegiate church of Boseham, where, it was alleged, the canons did nothing for the poor parishioners from the revenues they received. In his ordinances following the visitation the bishop required that this state of affairs be remedied. [49] The evidence from a visitation of ninety parishes in the diocese of Exeter in 1342 is similar; in all these parishes there was only one complaint of inadequate alms-giving. The parishioners at Ipplepene declared: "From time beyond memory down to the time of the present rector great and good hospitality used to be maintained both for rich and poor, and many other good works were done from the goods of the church, all of which have ceased altogether during the time of this rector." [50] Another example in the early fourteenth century comes from the diocese of Durham. When Bishop Richard de Kellawe passed through the parish of Wessingham the parishioners complained that the rector's agent did not keep hospitality or succor the poor or give alms in the parish as he ought. The bishop commanded that a portion of the church revenues be set aside for this purpose in the future. [51]

One cannot base any very dogmatic conclusions on the evidence available; but when parishioners who were prepared to bring all kinds of charges against their priests very seldom did raise the issue of neglect of the poor, the most obvious inference is that it was not a common failing among resident parsons and vicars. Perhaps Gasquet was not so far wrong when he wrote that the obligation "was fully accepted and carried out," and this, not because all priests were burning with zeal and Christian charity, but because, in refusing to give alms, they would have offended one of the strongest social conventions of the age. Even nowadays men will almost invariably give to a worthy cause if they are placed in a position where it is socially embarrassing to refuse. In the thirteenth century almsgiving by beneficed clerics was not regarded as a work of supererogation, to be expected from only the most zealous priests, but rather as the barest minimum that could be exacted even from those in other ways unworthy of their office. Thus Peckham ordered an absentee Bishop of Coventry to return to his diocese "in order that you, who are not adequate to minister spiritual things, may at least provide temporal goods for the poor." [52] And Grosseteste, protesting against the appointment of foreigners to benefices in England, complained that they "could not even take up residence to minister to the wants of the poor and to receive travellers." [53]

There is a passage in the chronicle of Matthew Paris which asserts that the provision of parochial poor relief was indeed a prevailing custom in thirteenth-century England: "Since a custom has heretofore prevailed and been observed in England that the rectors of parochial churches have always been remarkable for hospitality and have made a practice of supplying food to their parishioners who were in want, . . . if a portion of their benefices be taken away from them they will be under the necessity of refusing their hospitality. . . ." [54] The clergy who made this protest were arguing against a tax demanded by Pope Innocent IV in 1246, so their words should perhaps be taken with a grain of salt; they would naturally not seek to minimize their burdens on such an occasion. But it is hard to see how the argument could have been put forward in public at all if it was a matter of common knowledge that parochial poor relief was virtually nonexistent at this time, as is often said. Moreover, the same claim was reiterated on other similar occasions in the thirteenth century. [55]

Perhaps the strongest indication that poor relief was in actual practice commonly administered by parish priests is a negative one. Nearly all the numerous complaints about absenteeism, pluralities, and inadequately endowed vicarages mention the "diminution of hospitality" as a main ground of protest. A typical example is this from Bishop Newport of London, writing about absentee pluralists in 1318: "They neglect their cures . . . so that the threefold provision of the divine word, of good example, and of corporal sustenance of the needy is withdrawn altogether, divine worship is diminished, cure of souls neglected, and no hospitality is maintained. . . ." [56] This constant complaint seems inexplicable if, in any case, hospitality was generally neglected in parishes that did have resident priests. And, after all, the great majority of parishes were not appropriated or held by absentees by the end of the thirteenth century. The problem always is to get behind the clamor of protest about abuses to an understanding of the normal prevailing practice.

The evidence that can be adduced on the relation between legal theory and administrative practice is of its nature ambiguous. As Ashley pointed out, each new law that was enacted implied that the old law had not been fully effective, and it is inevitable that most of the evidence indicating that the law was enforced comes from instances where it was being broken. The interpretation of such evidence presents a delicate problem for the historian. It is the same problem that would face a research student five hundred years hence who set out to write a thesis on juvenile delinquency in the twentieth century. If he had at his disposal a selection of court records and the enactments of state legislatures and a number of newspaper discussions on the problem, but no precise statistics on the total amount of crime, he might well conclude that all the laws and administrative effort designed to combat delinquency in the twentieth century were quite ineffective. After all, people were complaining about it in the 1920's and they were still complaining in the 1950's and no doubt our researcher will be able to report that the complaints were just as loud in the 1990's. Having proved that the steps taken by society to combat delinquency were ineffective, he might then feel justified in assuming that practically all young persons were delinquent in the remote and barbaric age he was studying, just as Ashley assumed that practically all medieval parish priests were delinquent in fulfilling their canonical obligations. But the fact of the matter is that the vast majority of young people nowadays are not criminals. Juvenile delinquency arouses such continued public concern because there is far too much of it indeed, but also precisely because the instances involved are departures from a norm that is respected by the overwhelming majority.

So too it seems likely that the ecclesiastical law of the thirteenth century relating to poor relief was far too frequently broken, but that still the infractions represent departures from the norm, not the norm itself. In considering the very real abuses of absentee parsons and underendowed vicarages it must be borne in mind that their effect was counteracted to some extent by the great growth of endowed hospitals and almshouses in the thirteenth century, by private charity and the work of the guilds, and by the substantial doles of the monasteries. No serious medievalist nowadays believes in the "Golden Middle Ages" myth. We know too much about the stupidities and brutalities of that age to be impressed by word pictures of pious peasants perpetually dancing around Maypoles. But, in this particular matter, I am inclined to think that, taken all in all, the poor were better looked after in England in the thirteenth century than in any subsequent century until the present one. The only reservation we need make is that perhaps that is not saying much.

CHAPTER

VI The Later Middle Ages

The discussion of canonistic theory and administrative practice raises two further problems, which are both perhaps too complex to be dealt with adequately in a single short chapter, but certainly too important to be ignored altogether. If ecclesiastical poor law worked tolerably well in thirteenth-century England, why did it become so relatively ineffective in the later Middle Ages that, from the mid-fourteenth century on, the secular government became increasingly preoccupied with problems of poor relief? Again, what was the relationship between this new secular poor law and the pattern of canonistic thought and legislation on poor relief? Did it reflect a radically new attitude to poverty, or was it essentially an application by the secular government of the concepts that have already been discussed?

As for the first problem, there seem to be three main reasons for the growing inadequacy of the ecclesiastical poor law. For one thing, the problems of poor relief became very much more complex as a result of changes in the social and economic environment. Then, to an increasing degree, the administrative policies pursued by high ecclesiastical authorities hindered the effective working of the laws that existed, laws generally good in themselves if not altogether adequate in the changed circumstances. Finally, the canonists of the late fourteenth and the fifteenth centuries failed to display the intellectual vitality that was needed to devise new legal remedies for the new problems that arose.

The changes in economic environment affected both commerce and agriculture. The structure of international trade became more complex. More and more people earned their living as craftsmen, working for wages in trades that could be affected by dislocations in the market, perhaps caused by remote changes outside the knowledge or understanding of the workmen themselves. Still more important were the changes in rural life associated with the breakup of the manorial system, for, in spite of the growth of trade and towns, the vast majority of the working population in fifteenth-century England still lived by agriculture. In the "classical" manorial system the demesne land of the lord was cultivated by the forced labor of the villeins. The lord maintained his household from the produce of his estates; the villeins lived from the strips of land they held from the lord in return for labor services. The system was never either universal or static. All through the thirteenth century villeins sought, often successfully, to commute their labor services for money rents, while lords of manors sometimes found it convenient to lease out their demesne lands to some substantial farmer and thus become landlords living on fixed rents rather than on the direct exploitation of their own estates. And so, in agriculture as in commerce, there were developing a money economy and, associated with that, the beginnings of the whole modern apparatus of capital investment, credit, interest, and rent charges.[1] These were long-term changes, the working out of forces inherent in the economy and civilization of the Middle Ages, but the rate of change in the later Middle Ages and the impact of the whole process on problems of poor relief were profoundly influenced by the fortuitous calamity of the Black Death.

The Black Death, a virulent epidemic of bubonic plague, ravaged England in 1348–49 after sweeping through the countries of Continental Europe. It provides one of the few instances when the calamitous accounts of loss of life given by medieval chroniclers have been fully confirmed by modern research. Perhaps the loss in the first onset of the plague was not quite so high as has sometimes been supposed—the latest detailed investigation suggests a figure of about 25 per cent—but further damage arose from the fact that the plague remained endemic for two generations, producing an abnormally high death rate and a dwindling population. By 1400 the population of England was little more than half the preplague figure; it continued to decline until the second decade of the fifteenth century, and then only very slowly began to recover. Thus, superimposed on the normal pattern of economic evolution were all the dislocations produced by a rapidly declining population and then by a very slow rate of increase in an under-populated country.[2]

The most immediate and obvious effect of the plague was to create an unprecedented shortage of labor. Workmen demanded higher wages and villeins clamored to be free of their customary services so that they could take advantage of the favorable labor market. Landlords resisted these demands and governments sought to outlaw them with repressive legislation. This in turn contributed to a growing bitterness between the classes which produced serious peasant rebellions in England and elsewhere in the 1380's. The English rebels of 1381 were defeated and ruthlessly punished, but the impersonal play of economic forces obtained for the peasants in the end what they had not been able to win immediately by armed revolt. "No Act of Parliament could repeal the Black Death." When there was simply not enough labor to work all the formerly cultivated land the village serf had an effective reply to the lord who sought to exact rigorously the old irksome labor services—simply to desert the manor and migrate to a plague-devastated area where hard pressed landlords would be only too happy to hire him at high wages, with no questions asked.[3]

Hence a striking feature of social life in the century after the Black Death was a greatly increased fluidity of labor. The plague struck capriciously; some districts were hardly touched while in others there was a critical shortage of workers. The dwindling population throughout Europe led to a general depression of trade, so that in the crafts affected there could be temporary local unemployment even amid a general labor shortage.[4] There was never a time when so many men had such strong incentives to wander away from their towns and villages to try to better their condition, and the roads became filled with vagrants looking for work or for loot or lured by promises of fabulously high wages in the depopulated parts of the country. Other factors contributed to this growth of vagrancy, for the century after the Black Death was a period of extensive military campaigning. The Hundred Years' War was far more devastating in its effects on France than on England, but even in England there were thousands of soldiers discharged after every major campaign, and many of them would not have found it easy to go back to the immemorial monotony of village life. Some would go to swell the bands of vagabonds, half-beggars, half-bandits, who were beginning to infest the country-side. The number involved was no doubt very small in relation to the total population, but it may have been significant in relation to the fringe of wandering beggars, for the growth among that class of even a small core of reckless marauders, trained in the use of arms, and not likely to shrink from shedding blood, could have made the whole problem of vagrancy seem increasingly formidable. The homeless wanderer was becoming an object of fear and suspicion as well as of pity.

In the fifteenth century yet another economic factor tended to increase the number of vagrants. This was the enclosure of arable land for sheep farming, which sometimes led to the eviction of whole village populations. The latest study of the subject suggests that such evictions were more widespread and occurred at an earlier period than economic historians have generally supposed.[5] Once again, the numbers involved must have been very small in relation to the whole population but not necessarily insignificant in relation to the fringe of hungry vagabonds.

It would be misleading to suggest that these changes led to any general deterioration in the position of the peasants as a class. Certainly the reverse was true. Although short-term economic dislocations could produce all kinds of anomalies, the dominant factor over the whole period was the shortage of labor. Faced with untilled fields or rotting harvests, the lords had to make the best bargains they could, and, in the long run, the bargains usually brought to an end the old servile burdens. By the end of the fifteenth century serfdom had become almost extinct in England. Yet it is no very unusual paradox that an age which saw a general rise in the status and living standards of most of the peasantry was also vexed with new problems of poverty. In the nineteenth century wealth accumulated at an unprecedented rate, and that century saw a great improvement in the position of the laboring classes as a whole; it also saw an exceptional degree of preoccupation with problems of destitution and poor relief. It seems that long periods of economic change and instability necessarily aggravate the problems of the small minority at the very bottom of the economic scale even when their general tendency is to improve the lot of the working population as a whole. Most villeins who left their holdings to become laborers at high wages probably improved their economic position, but the odd individuals among them who were crippled through sickness or accident might find themselves at a worse disadvantage than ever. So, too, the old and impotent who had found some security in the customary manorial law of tenure and inheritance were probably less protected as the whole manorial system decayed. Most important of all, the economic changes of the later Middle Ages meant that from mid-fourteenth century on, the problem of relieving poverty became inextricably intertwined with the problem of suppressing vagrancy. That circumstance conditioned the whole tone and temper of secular legislation in the field of poor relief.

Before turning to this secular legislation we have to consider

the response of the ecclesiastical authorities to the problems we
have outlined. That response seems to have been inadequate both
on the level of administrative action and on the level of legal
theory. It is obvious enough that, in the new conditions, the
canonical obligation of beneficed clerics to "keep hospitality" without encouraging the willfully idle became more than ever a
complex yet crucial task. But, at this time, when it was so particularly important that parish revenues should be husbanded and
wisely employed, they were in fact dissipated in a more barefaced
fashion than before through the twin abuses of appropriations and
absenteeism.

There were new laws, and good laws, against these abuses in
the fourteenth century. In 1317 Pope John XXII promulgated
the decree *Execrabilis,* which defined in detail the basic principle
that no man should hold two benefices with cure of souls, and in
1366 Pope Urban V decreed that no further appropriations should
take place without papal approval. But, in fact, papal dispensations
were granted so readily that the laws might almost as well not
have existed. Their main result perhaps was that they enhanced
the opportunities of the popes to derive financial profit from con-
doning malpractices; the situation has been described, fairly enough,
as a "systematization of simony." [6] Certainly the holding of parishes
by absentee pluralists did increase in the fifteenth century in spite
of the decree of 1366. Again, at a time when it was particularly
essential for the bishops to attempt some sort of coördination of
the charitable activities of their dioceses, the tendency was for
more and more of the greater hospitals to acquire exemption from
episcopal control, and, in spite of the decree *Quia Contingit,* all
too often a major part of their revenues came to be diverted
from the real purpose of the foundation to provide a handsome
income for its administrators. Every medieval Barchester had its
Hiram's Hospital.

There is no great mystery in the apparent ability of wealthy
ecclesiastical institutions to conduct their affairs in a fashion evidently opposed to the spirit of the canon law. The law laid down,
for instance, that appropriations of parishes to monasteries were
to be permitted only in certain exceptional circumstances. But the

individual monastery, seeking an appropriation, could hire expensive lawyers to prove that the circumstances were indeed exceptional, and it might also enlist the support of a powerful lay patron to ensure a favorable judgment in a borderline case. The persistent intervention of the king himself on behalf of the priory of Worcester in 1307 is an extreme example.[7] The parishioners, who stood to lose by the appropriation of their parish revenues, were seldom in a position to bring such pressures to bear. The situation is, after all, familiar enough in contemporary government. In modern terms, evasions of laws designed to promote the public welfare were being condoned as a result of vigorous "lobbying" by private interests. Only an incorrupt and very vigilant administration can resist pressures of that sort consistently. But ecclesiastical administration in the later Middle Ages was lacking in vitality and pastoral zeal on every level from parish to Papacy.

There was a great shortage of priests after the Black Death, and many were given charge of parishes who would not have been considered qualified for such positions even according to the far from exacting standards that had prevailed up to then. Incidentally, after the plague men of private means formed a much lower proportion of new ordinands than before.[8] English bishops in the late fourteenth and the fifteenth centuries were very commonly royal servants, who were raised to the episcopate as a reward for distinguished work in the king's administration. They tended to be able, rather worldly men, not guilty of any flagrant dereliction of duty or scandalous misconduct, but they were preoccupied with affairs other than the pastoral care of souls which ought to have been their first concern as bishops. At the head of the hierarchy, the Papacy was in no state to recall its subordinates to a proper sense of their duties. The popes of the eleventh and twelfth centuries had embarked on a program of ecclesiastical centralization in order to combat abuses that were widespread throughout the Church, but by the fourteenth and fifteenth centuries the process had produced such an elaborate bureaucracy that merely to keep it functioning became an almost all-absorbing task for the most energetic pontiff. The centralization that began as a means to an

end produced a machinery of government whose continued running
became virtually an end in itself. Altogether, the complaints about
neglect of parish poor relief, which become loud, frequent, and
bitter at the end of the fourteenth century, were, from one point of
view, only a minor symptom of a general decay in standards of
ecclesiastical administration in the later Middle Ages.

In the development of canonistic theory on poor relief there
seems again to have been a failure of adequate response to the
conditions that were emerging in the century after the Black
Death. It used to be the fashion to decry all late medieval thought
as mere sterile pedantry, a realm of labyrinthine gloom, its shadows
only accentuated by the lucid dawn of the Renaissance. Nowadays
the fashion has changed. Fourteenth- and fifteenth-century theologians are studied with sympathy, and precursors of modern
physical science are being discovered at a remarkable rate among
the philosophers of that age. Even among the canonists, students
of economic thought have discovered much subtle speculation
on problems of commercial morality, revolving around the doctrine
of usury, and apparently inspired by the developing capitalism of
the fifteenth century.[9] And yet there is something in the old
point of view. Fifteenth-century commentaries are usually enormous
tomes, inflated beyond all measure in order to display the pre-
tentious erudition of the author, and it does not always happen
that there is some pearl of original thought concealed beneath
the shell of accumulated authorities. Indeed, so far as my own
experience goes, there is nothing quite like a fifteenth-century
canon-law treatise to give the undiluted flavor of decadent scho-
lasticism.

Such criticism may not be valid for the canonists' approach to
economic problems as a whole, but it does seem justified in respect
to their treatment of problems of poor relief. It was not that they
ceased to discuss such problems. On the contrary, famous canonists
like Panormitanus, Joannes de Turrecremata, Dominicus de Sancto
Gemignano, and Felinus de Sandeus continued to discuss with the
most patient erudition all the abstract issues about property and
charity, with more and more finespun distinctions and more and
more citations of earlier authorities. For instance, Joannes de

Turrecremata's commentary on *Distinctio* 86 of the *Decretum* amounts to a solid treatise of fifteen folio pages on poor law principles.[10] It is all sound traditional stuff; indeed the only complaint one can make about it is that there is nothing there that could not just as well have been written two centuries earlier. A carping critic might add that everything of importance that Joannes had to say could have been said very adequately in about a fifth of the space.

In spite of all that has recently been written on the changing pattern of economic activity and the changing climate of economic thought at the end of the Middle Ages, these writers do not reveal any significant reorientation of outlook on problems concerning the relief of poverty. The sin of avarice was condemned as vigorously as ever.[11] The testimony of a poor man was not to be rejected in a court of law, it was pointed out, because poverty was not in itself dishonorable.[12] Sometimes it was added that the poor were subject to greater temptations than the rich, sometimes that it was easier for them to save their souls since they did not have such exacting responsibilities; both lines of thought were entirely traditional. The basic obligation of the rich to the poor was commonly defined in the formula that had been accepted two centuries earlier: a man who possessed "superfluities" was morally bound to give to all in need, and those who had adequate though not "superfluous" means were bound to give to all in a state of "extreme necessity." [13] The canonists continued to interest themselves in defining the limits of ecclesiastical jurisdiction over poor men's cases, but again they merely rehearsed arguments of the thirteenth century in discussing the question.[14] They also continued to specify in considerable detail the privileges that could be claimed by poor litigants pleading before church courts, but here too they were merely elaborating on principles established centuries earlier.[15]

Again, these fifteenth-century canonists continued to teach that one of the obligations of an ecclesiastical benefice was to provide funds for poor relief. Panormitanus and Antonius de Burgos both observed that clerics could be compelled to exercise hospitality because "it is certain that benefices were principally instituted for this work of mercy." [16] But in other contexts Panormitanus struck a less affirmative note, insisting that the obligation to the poor had only third priority in the claims on a benefice. First the priest was to be adequately supported, then the church adequately maintained, and only then, if there was something left over, could the poor claim a share.[17]

As to the issue that really became crucial from the fifteenth century on, the problem of discrimination in charity, the canonists once again repeated old doctrines faithfully enough, but without any attempt to formulate a new response to the problems of their own times.[18] Joannes de Turrecremata dismissed the central problem of the able-bodied poor in a curt couple of lines; a man who could work with his hands was not to be numbered among the poor, he wrote, but rather was to be rebuked as a defrauder of the poor if he sought alms.[19] But Joannes devoted a full column and a half to the apparently far more fascinating problem of whether a man ought to give alms first to an infidel father or a faithful stranger. Once more the twelfth-century jest of Petrus Manducator was solemnly disinterred, together with the comments of Huguccio, Raymundus de Pennaforte, Goffredus Tranensis, Hostiensis, and Gulielmus Durandus, and, after all this huffing and puffing, the traditional conclusion was arrived at yet again. The erring father came first. Then a few pages further on, as though feeling that he had not fully done justice to himself, Joannes lavished another folio column on the same point.[20] The statement by Panormitanus that "civil law and canon law both condemn public begging without evident cause of necessity" does seem for a moment to catch the authentic flavor of an age beset by problems of vagrancy and "valiant beggars," but in fact Panormitanus was consciously recalling the doctrine set out by Joannes Teutonicus in his *Glossa Ordinaria* to the *Decretum*, and he carried the argument no further than had his thirteenth-century predecessor.[21]

Although the canonists of the thirteenth century had shown a good deal of alertness to the problems of their age, there were some important questions that they neglected. For instance, they never seem to have discussed in detail how the poor relief efforts of a parish priest ought to be divided between the needs of his own parishioners and those of poor travelers. The whole medieval idea that charity should begin within the individual himself, and then spread out in circles as it were, first to his own family, then to other dependents, then to strangers, implied that, other things being equal, a priest's first duty was to his own parishioners to whom he stood as spiritual father. The English local legislation makes it clear that this was indeed taken for granted, and in the fourteenth century John of Ayton put the point explicitly: "Note the argument that revenues of parish churches are owed to the poor parishioners rather than to outsiders . . . which I believe to be true unless the outsider should be in greater need." [22] But beyond that the canonists seem never to have considered the issue. Perhaps it did not seem particularly important in the thirteenth century, but it was desperately important in the fifteenth century when the whole problem of relieving poverty had become entangled with the problem of suppressing vagrancy, and still the canonists did not consider it adequately.

What was really needed by the fifteenth century was a kind of scholastic critique of employability in able-bodied vagrants. It was no longer enough to divide beggars into the impotent and the able-bodied; the real problem that was emerging was to distinguish among the able-bodied themselves. There were those who were downright idle, those who were eager and willing to work but could find no work, those who would not work on the old terms and had left their villages looking for better conditions elsewhere, those who were in temporary need between spells of casual labor; and for each category there were subsidiary questions to be considered regarding the eligibility for help of their wives and children. In view of the almost fantastic fertility of the canonists in elaborating distinctions and subdistinctions on subjects that really interested them, it is not at all difficult to imagine a page or two of argumentation along these lines. But such an analysis does not seem to have been undertaken. The canonists' method of argument lent itself conveniently to such an approach and the circumstances of the time demanded it, but it might not have been easy to find "authorities" for all the points involved.

The thirteenth-century canonists on the whole give the impression that they were interested in interpreting old texts in the light of current needs. But the fifteenth-century writers seem too often to have been interested only in interpreting old texts in the light of other old texts.

Since we have been dealing mainly with conditions in England, it will be appropriate to illustrate further the climate of opinion among the fifteenth-century canonists by bringing together the comments on poor law of a famous English jurist of that age, William Lyndwood.[23] In 1443 Lyndwood produced his *Provinciale*, a collection of the canons of the English provincial councils, arranged in the same fashion as the volumes of decretals in the *Corpus Iuris Canonici*, and equipped with an extensive commentary which interpreted the English canons in the light of the general legislation of the Church and the glosses of the major canonists. Lyndwood's own commentary exemplifies in typical fashion both the achievement of the fifteenth-century canonists in preserving a great body of sound traditional doctrine, and also their occasional lack of enterprise in coping with contemporary issues.

His first comments on poor relief were evoked by Archbishop Langton's decree in the Council of Oxford (1222) declaring that prelates should have worthy almoners and should make themselves available to hear poor men's cases. On the latter point, Lyndwood explained that ecclesiastical judges ought to be especially prompt to hear the cases of poor litigants, since otherwise the poor might suffer oppression, having nothing to offer, "for justice is swiftly violated with gold." He also considered the precise meaning of the word "poor" in this connection. It might mean anyone who labored for his living or it might mean anyone whose property was worth less than fifty gold pieces, but Lyndwood thought that the best definition was simply a man who could not afford to pay for legal assistance. He added that the bishop should not only ensure that such people received a hearing but that they were provided with legal counsel too.[24]

Lyndwood's comments on other words in Langton's decree opened up the major themes concerning poverty and charity which he elaborated in more detail in subsequent glosses. In his explanation of the word *eleemosynarios* (almoners), he took occasion to restate the standard doctrine on the obligation of almsgiving. In general, "spiritual alms" (prayer and teaching) were better than mere corporal alms, but there were occasions when corporal alms were more important—if a man was hungry it was better to feed him than to teach him. As for the obligation to give alms, some said that this was merely a matter of counsel, others that it was a matter of precept. According to Lyndwood the latter point of view was correct when a man possessed superfluities or the applicant was in a state of extreme need.[25] He also explained in detail what was meant by "extreme need."[26] On the word *hospitales* in Langton's decree, Lyndwood commented that all priests ought to be hospitable "because, as Jerome says, the houses of the clergy should be common to all." But there were two kinds of hospitality. The first was hospitality inspired by Christian charity; the second was hospitality that could be demanded of an inferior as a servile burden. It was hospitality of the first kind that priests were bound to provide. If they had sufficient resources they were to give to all in need; if there was not enough for all they should follow the Ambrosian system of preferences set out in *Distinctio* 86 of the *Decretum*.[27]

Lyndwood had a number of comments on the canons that required absentee rectors to make provision for the poor of their parishes. Peckham's law of 1281 laid down that "rectors who do not reside in their churches nor have vicars shall display the grace of hospitality through their agents,"[28] and in 1342 Archbishop Stratford decreed that monks who held appropriated parishes should distribute each year "a quantity of alms to be assessed by the bishops . . . to the poor parishioners of those benefices." Lyndwood called attention to a technical difference in the wording of these decrees:

In this monks having appropriated churches differ from other rectors who do not reside. For such rectors are held to provide hospitality in the place of their benefice, especially for poor parishioners in a state of extreme need. . . . But the monks are not obliged to provide this kind of hospitality, but to distribute alms in money. . . .[29]

This distinction seems to raise one of the central issues of poor relief policy, but Lyndwood did not undertake any further discussion of it. From the sixteenth century to the twentieth poor law administrators have debated the relative merits of "outdoor relief," the allotment of a maintenance allowance to paupers in their own homes, and "indoor relief," the provision of shelter as well as food by the relieving authorities. By commenting on the usage in different laws of the terms *hospitalitas* and *eleemosyna*, Lyndwood called attention to the two different modes of procedure, but the absence of all further comment makes it clear that he was merely concerned to emphasize a legal technicality, and was not interested in the broader issues involved.

Besides pointing out that all cases of extreme need were to be relieved, Lyndwood also attempted on several occasions to define the precise arithmetical proportion of the parish revenues that ought to be devoted to the relief of the poor. His comments provide a useful corrective for those who imagine that in England, all through the Middle Ages, the poor were legally entitled to precisely one-third of the tithes, and that only the wickedness and greed of the clerics prevented them from getting it. In different contexts Lyndwood suggested as suitable proportions a half, a quarter, a fifth, and a sixth. As it happens, a third is about the only possibility that he did not mention. And his final conclusion was the usual one, that there could be no fixed proportion, enforceable in all circumstances, since the amount needed varied according to local conditions. It was to be assessed, he wrote, according to the resources of the church and the quality and needs of the incumbent of the benefice, and with regard paid too to the numbers and neediness of the poor to be supported.[30]

Another of Lyndwood's comments on this theme has a special interest because it became the focal point of a sharp little controversy about the endowment of English benefices in the fifteenth century. After explaining that churches near busy roads required greater revenues than those in remote places because of the greater expenses of hospitality, Lyndwood wrote:

. . . unde ulterius dotari debent ecclesiae in Anglia, ubi requiruntur majores expensae quam in Provincia, ubi sufficiunt expensae minores. Faciunt ad hoc *no. per Jo. in no. de praebe. c. cum secundum. ver. quantitate.*

That is,

> . . . whence churches in England, where greater expenses are required, ought to be better endowed than in Provence where lesser expenses suffice.

The concluding reference was to the *Novella ad Decretales* of Joannes Andreae.

Gasquet used this passage as evidence that benefices in England were adequately endowed to meet the expenses of hospitality: "This [hospitality] according to Lyndwood was well understood and practised in England, where the churches, to meet those calls, were better endowed than they were abroad." [31] Coulton indignantly protested that Gasquet had grossly distorted and even reversed the sense of his text: "When, for instance, Lyndwood says that the clergy *'ought to be better endowed'* in order to cope with the problem of poor relief, Cardinal Gasquet translates this as *'are well endowed'*; and he summarizes Lyndwood's main comment with equal inaccuracy." [32] Coulton printed this criticism over and over again. Gasquet, as usual, never deigned to reply; but in fact he was not seriously at fault, and, on this occasion, Coulton is rather the more misleading of the two. Lyndwood did not write that English benefices "ought to be better endowed" than they actually were, as Coulton implied, but that they ought to be better endowed than benefices in Provence, which is something quite different.

Neither Coulton nor Gasquet sought to explain the reference to Provence, though it might have seemed odd to them that an English bishop should quite gratuitously animadvert on conditions in a remote part of Christendom. The explanation is obvious enough if we remember that there was one very famous medieval canonist who did have an intimate knowledge of both countries. That was Hostiensis, who spent several years in England in the service of King Henry III around the year 1240 and subsequently became Bishop of Sisteron in Provence. [33] Hostiensis' great *Commentaria* on the Decretals contains the original source of Lyndwood's comment, which Lyndwood had borrowed from Joannes Andreae, who in turn referred back to Hostiensis. Benefices were to be endowed, Joannes wrote, "according to the quality of the person and of the district, so that more is assigned in England than in Provence even when the persons are equal, according to Hostiensis." [34] Thus, when Lyndwood came to write that benefices ought to be more wealthy in England than in Provence there was no implication that in fact they were not more wealthy, still less that they ought to be wealthier than they actually were. He was taking it for granted that his readers knew the familiar canonistic tag asserting that English benefices were better endowed than Provençal ones, and was making the point that, moreover, they *ought* to be better endowed because of the greater expenses of hospitality in England.

In view of all that is known of appropriations, pluralities, and absenteeism in fifteenth-century England, it is a little surprising to find a contemporary who was an active diocesan administrator as well as a canonist writing thus complacently about the ability of English benefices to sustain the burden of hospitality. Perhaps the most significant feature of the whole gloss is the fact that when, in mid-fifteenth century, Lyndwood wished to allude to the endowment of the churches in England to make a point in a canonistic argument, he did not refer to his own ample experience, but preferred to quote the observation of an Italian canonist of the fourteenth century, who in turn relied on the testimony of another Italian canonist of the thirteenth century. Incidentally, one would never gather from reading Lyndwood's glosses that there was an acute problem of vagabondage in the England of his day, or that there existed any need to harmonize the law of the Church on hospitality with the law of the state on suppression of vagrancy.

Another text of Lyndwood's calls for examination, both because it too has been misinterpreted and because it seems related to an important trend of thought among other contemporary canonists. In discussing Archbishop Stratford's canon on poor relief funds in appropriated parishes, Lyndwood considered in great detail the precise nature of the legal rights that poor parishioners derived from it, and how those rights could legally be enforced.[35] What if the bishop failed to assess the quantity of alms to be distributed in an appropriated parish? Either he could be compelled by the archbishop, wrote Lyndwood, or, if he persisted in his negligence, the archbishop himself could make the assessment. But once the assessment was made, did it provide the parishioners with grounds for a legal action in the event of default in payment? The problem here was that only a determinate person could bring suit, and the phrase "poor parishioners" seemed too vague to provide a basis for an action by any individual. Lyndwood pointed out that if there existed a corporate group of poor persons in the parish— he probably had in mind a hospital[36]—it could sue as a recognized legal person. Even if there was no such institution, Lyndwood thought that the law would regard the poor parishioners of a given place as a sufficiently determinate group to bring suit, just as a will in favor of "the poor" would be held valid although it failed to specify a determinate heir. But he suggested that, to be on the safe side, the parishioners would do better to appeal to "the office of the judge," that is, to resort to an established equitable procedure by which an ecclesiastical superior could be invoked to rectify an injustice. There was no ambiguity at all in Lyndwood's view that the poor did have legal rights and that, by one process or the other, those rights could be enforced in the courts.[37]

The other fifteenth-century canonists who considered the problem of how the poor could obtain legal enforcement of their canonical rights, especially the right to support, approached it from a different angle. Lyndwood explained in unusual detail how the parishioners might proceed against the absentee holder of a benefice, but everyone agreed in principle that the holder of a benefice did have a legally enforceable obligation toward the poor. Several other canonists about this time took up the more controversial question whether ordinary lay folk could be legally compelled to contribute to the support of the poor. There was no doubt at all that everyone who possessed superfluous wealth was under a moral obligation to help those in need; the canonists dwelt upon that fact over and over again. A man who refused to do so committed a sin and could be refused absolution in confession unless he promised to mend his ways. All that was common ground. The debatable question was whether the obligation was enforceable through a legal action, or through legal coercion by public authority, outside the private and sacramental relationship between penitent and confessor.

The point was already being discussed around 1200. The English canonist John of Tynemouth wrote; "We are obliged [*tenemur*] to do many things that we are not compelled to do," and he cited the precept "Feed the starving" as a case in point.[38] But, as we have seen, Joannes Teutonicus held that the rich could in fact be legally compelled to give to the poor if the procedure of *denunciatio evangelica* was invoked (the same procedure that Lyndwood was to suggest in dealing with his parallel problem). The same view was held by several other distinguished canonists who were contemporaries of Joannes, including Huguccio, Alanus, and the author of the *Glossa Palatina*.[39] It was repeated in the next generation by Bernardus Parmensis in his *Glossa Ordinaria* to the Decretals when he commented on a law requiring parish priests to admonish their parishioners that they should be hospitable and should not cheat travelers by charging them high prices for provisions. Referring to the earlier view, Bernardus commented on the word *hospitales:* "For they can be compelled to this by excommunication."[40] But this position did not go unchallenged and, indeed, after Bernardus Parmensis it seems to have fallen out of favor for nearly two centuries.

In the mid-thirteenth century Innocent IV cited the earlier opinion but held that it was not valid unless a notorious scandal was involved.[41] Hostiensis maintained without qualification that the duty to be hospitable, which he interpreted in the broadest sense, could not be enforced by external coercion, even though it was binding in conscience:

The meaning is this, that priests ought to admonish their parishioners about two things. First, that they should be hospitable, good almsgivers and charitable toward the poor, for it is not enough that they pay tithes in full unless they give alms from the other nine parts; and second that they should not sell more dearly [to travelers]. . . . But as to the hospitality both priests and bishops shall content themselves with admonition. As to the selling, bishops can apply coercion.[42]

In the fourteenth century the *Glossa Ordinaria* to the *Extravagantes Joannis XXII* taught that the precise difference between beneficed clerics and others in this matter was that the obligation of the clerics was legally enforceable, while that of other men was not.[43] Henricus de Bohic was of the same opinion.[44]

Then, in the fifteenth century, there was another change in learned opinion. Petrus de Ancharano, at the very beginning of the century, cited both earlier points of view without committing himself,[45] but later on Dominicus de Sancto Gemignano, Panormitanus, Felinus de Sandeus, and Stephanus de Gaeta all reviewed the problem and all returned to the early thirteenth-century view that a man who refused to give alms could be denounced to the bishop and compelled to give.[46] At the beginning of the sixteenth century Antonius de Burgos reported that this was the common opinion of commentators everywhere.[47] This reorientation of thought is perhaps the one contribution of the fifteenth-century canonists which is of major importance in the general history of poor law. It seems especially significant coming on the eve of the various schemes for compulsory poor relief contributions which were advocated in the sixteenth century.

The procedure of *denunciatio evangelica* which the canonists recommended to enforce contributions had especially interesting repercussions in English law. It has lately been argued that this canonical procedure provided the foundation upon which was built up the whole system of equity jurisdiction in the court of chancery; [48] and, in the field of English secular poor law, there seems an echo of the canonists' doctrine in the act "for the provision and relief of the poor" of 1552. This statute laid down that alms for the poor were to be collected in each parish church and that, if anyone "obstinately and frowardly" refused to give, he was to be reported to the bishop who should "send for him or them to induce and persuade him or them by charitable ways and means, and so, according to his discretion, to take order for the reformation thereof." [49] There is quite a change of tone, however, in the secular law. The canonists would have expected the bishop to judge and command, not merely to induce and persuade.

We are now in a position to review the whole question of the relationship between canonical jurisprudence and the developing secular poor law from the fourteenth century to the sixteenth, concentrating once again on the English tradition. The prevailing opinion seems to be that at some point there was a breakdown in a relatively ineffective medieval system which was in due course followed by the construction of a new system of secular poor law based on novel principles. But everyone seems to have a different opinion as to when the old system "broke down." According to the earlier writers the administration of parochial relief according to canonical principles had virtually ceased by the mid-twelfth century. But Hartridge tells us that a petition of the Commons in the Parliament of 1391 "is a sweeping indictment of a complete break-down of the parish relief." And Coulton calls attention to an archidiaconal visitation of Oxfordshire in 1520 which covered 193 parishes, noting that "neglect of parochial hospitality or almsgiving was reported from thirty-five parishes." [50] This is cited, of course, as evidence of the inadequacy of the parish relief system at the beginning of the sixteenth century. But a corollary of the figures given is that an archidiaconal visitation which was paying serious attention to the provision of parochial poor relief found conditions tolerably satisfactory in 158 of the 193 parishes. Modern poor relief administrators may feel that this was not too bad a score.

The truth is, of course, that the canonical system of poor relief never did "break down" in medieval England. In spite of its growing imperfections, it survived into the sixteenth century to provide a foundation for the secular poor law of the Tudors (which also incorporated other elements derived from theorists like Vives and from the examples of Continental reformers). The elements of continuity and of change in English poor law can be illustrated from the provisions of the major secular statutes in this field from the middle of the fourteenth century on. The first reaction to the Black Death was the Ordinance of Laborers of 1349. Its main purpose was to prevent laborers wandering away from their work to seek higher wages, and, to render this provision effective, it forbade the giving of alms to able-bodied beggars under pain of imprisonment "so that thereby they may be compelled to labor for their necessary living." [51] An act of 1388 laid down more specific rules to prevent laborers leaving their place of work, and provided for the punishment of able-bodied beggars, but it also acknowledged by implication that those incapable of working should be allowed to beg. Even impotent beggars, however, were forbidden to wander as vagrants; they were required to remain in the town where they were living at the time the act was promulgated, or to settle in a neighboring place, or to return to the place of their birth. [52] In these provisions lies the germ of the whole future law of settlement.

Three years later, in 1391, there came a statute of a very different sort:

Because divers damages and hindrances sometimes have happened, and daily do happen to the parishioners of divers places by the appropriation of benefices of the same places, it is agreed and assented . . . that the diocesan of the place upon appropriation of such churches shall ordain, according to the value of such churches, a convenient sum of money to be paid and distributed yearly . . . to the poor parishioners of the said churches, in aid of their living and sustenance for ever; and also that the vicar be well and sufficiently endowed. [53]

This, of course, was merely using the authority of the secular government to secure more effective enforcement of the existing canon law. It has usually been maintained that the first activities of the state in the field of poor law were almost entirely negative and repressive, and revealed scarcely a hint of the need for some public relief of the destitute which was later acknowledged in the Tudor laws. But the acts of 1388 and 1391 must be considered together. Fourteenth-century parliaments were quite aware that a system of public poor relief was necessary, but they did not seek to create one by statute because they assumed that such a system already existed and was adequately defined in the canon law of the Church. When it became evident that the canon law was being broken too flagrantly, Parliament acted to ensure its more effective enforcement.

Even the "negative" measures adopted by Parliament during

this period were generally in accordance with the teachings of church lawyers. The canonists had quite consistently held that able-bodied beggars were to be denied alms in order that they should not be encouraged in idleness. The secular laws against vagrancy as such seem more original, for there had been no detailed canonical legislation on this subject (except for numerous decrees against vagabond clerics). But the canonists certainly disapproved of vagrancy in principle. They taught, for instance, that a wife could properly refuse to live with a husband who became a vagabond; the seriousness of the issue is indicated by the fact that they did not regard leprosy in a husband as a sufficient reason to justify his wife's leaving him.[54] There seems no reason why the canonists should not have accepted the new vagrancy laws as quite in accordance with their own attitude.

The laws against vagrancy and against abuses in appropriated churches were reënacted during the fifteenth century, and there were also laws against the "depopulation" of villages by evictions, but there were no major new departures in the principles of the poor law itself until the act of 1531. This statute again enacted severe penalties against vagrants, but it also required justices of the peace to register the names of all "aged, poor and impotent persons," and to give them licenses to beg within a defined district.[55] A much more positive approach is reflected in the act of 1536, which provided for regular collections on behalf of the poor to be made in parish churches, and also laid down that the parish funds available could be used, not only for the support of the impotent, but also to provide work for "such as be lusty or having their limbs strong enough to labor."[56] This act, so J. R. Tanner wrote, was "mainly concerned with the application of a new principle—the legal responsibility of each parish for the relief of its own poor" by "an authorised and systematic collection of alms." The principle of parochial responsibility was really a very old one; Grosseteste and Peckham had acknowledged it in the thirteenth century; the only novelty is that we find it now in an act of Parliament instead of in an ecclesiastical canon. Again, canon law ever since the thirteenth century had urged the parishioners as well as the parson to contribute to the support of the poor, and the emergence of the compulsory rating schemes in fifteenth-century English parishes, which the Webbs noted as providing immediate precedents for the Tudor law of parish relief, seems to have coincided precisely with the reorientation of canonistic thought concerning the legality of enforcing such contributions. It seems that in practice in the fifteenth century the emphasis shifted from the contribution of the resident priest to the contribution of the parishioners, and this was a natural adjustment within the framework of established law for an age when benefices were often improverished, and villagers generally more prosperous than before.

The act of 1536 did not provide that the giving of alms could be enforced by law, but another act of 1552 contained the provision, previously mentioned, for denouncing to the bishop a man who refused to give, and Elizabeth's act of 1563 finally laid down that, if the bishop's exhortations were unsuccessful, a compulsory contribution could be assessed and collected under pain of imprisonment.[57] Tanner again referred to these provisions of 1552 and 1563 as "a novel provision" and "a new departure," but they were in essence only adaptations of a procedure that the canonists had recommended as far back as the late twelfth century. The system of denouncing recalcitrant parishioners to the ecclesiastical authorities seems to have been widely used all through the reign of Elizabeth, even after the act of 1572 had provided for regular compulsory poor rate assessments to be made by the justices of the peace.[58]

In the sixteenth century the state absorbed the Church in England, and the system of dual coequal authorities which was characteristic of the Middle Ages came to an end. In taking over the Church the state necessarily became responsible for the system of public poor relief which until then had been regulated by canon law, and which was in fact badly in need of reform. The reform was undertaken with considerable vigor, but it retained many essential features of the old system; Tudor poor law was in the main a legitimate development of the canonistic tradition, not a negation of it. In recent years, many scholars have been engaged in building bridges across the gulf that was once supposed to separate the "Middle Ages" from the "Renaissance." It seems that in many fields of life and thought there were elements of continuity at least as important as the elements of change; and that proves true in the history of poor law too. From the reception of Gratian's *Decretum* in the mid-twelfth century to the final codification of the Elizabethan poor law in 1601, a single developing tradition without any sudden break or reversal of policy can be traced. Even the substitution of secular coercion for ecclesiastical coercion was a gradual business; the process began in the fourteenth century and was not quite complete by the end of Elizabeth's reign.

Such reference to a single developing tradition ought perhaps to stress the word "developing." The Tudor legislation was certainly no mere reënactment of the old canon law with more effective provisions for its enforcement. On the contrary, sixteenth-century legislators were as alert and responsive to the practical problems of their own age as the canonists had been in their best days. But the really new departures in Tudor poor law were not the things that are usually singled out for emphasis in discussions on its novelty. The acknowledgment that society had to provide for the impotent poor through established public authority, the rule that each parish should support its own poor, the principle of compulsory poor relief contributions—all these things were old and canonical. The most important new element in Tudor poor law, apart from the changes in administrative machinery, lay in its attempts to develop a constructive approach to the problem of the able-bodied unemployed from 1536 onward; and, likewise, the greatest defect in canonistic theories of poor relief at the end of the Middle Ages was their failure to deal with this problem. If the secular laws against vagabonds from the fourteenth century on seem excessively harsh in their treatment of men who were sometimes genuinely unemployed, the canonists must bear some share of the blame in that they, who by tradition and training were best fitted to analyze such a problem, failed to provide adequate guidance in the matter.

Yet in spite of all the imperfections in canonistic theory and in medieval practice it is still heartening to reflect that, in a civilization quite different from ours, men meditated on the problems of poverty and came to the conclusions that "poverty is not a kind of crime," that "in case of doubt it is better to do too much than to do nothing at all," above all that the intrinsic human dignity of a poor man was to be respected by those who sought to help him: "A poor man is an honorable person." The decay of medieval poor relief could provide two lessons of a more negative sort. The first is that no system of poor law, however well drafted, can achieve good results if administrative policies rub against the grain of the law, against its spirit and intention; the second is that a theory of poor relief, to be effective, must be flexible, not fossilized, continuously adapted in its practical applications to changes in the social and economic environment within which it operates. Such lessons are as relevant for the twentieth century as for the fifteenth.

Notes

Abbreviations

I. CORPUS IURIS CANONICI

Clem.	*Clementis Papae Quinti Constitutiones* (Paris, 1601)
Decretum	*Decretum Gratiani* (Paris, 1601)
Extrav. Jo. XXII	*Constitutiones Ioannis Papae XXII* (Paris, 1601)
Sext.	*Liber Sextus Decretalium Bonifacii Papae VIII* (Paris, 1601)
X.	*Decretales Gregorii Papae IX* (Paris, 1601) ("X." was a conventional abbreviation for *Liber Extra*, an alternative title for the Gregorian Decretals)

The canons of the *Decretum* were divided partly into *distinctiones* and partly into *causae*, which were subdivided into *quaestiones*. Its texts are cited thus: *Dist.*42 c.2 refers to the second canon of *Distinctio* 42; C.12 q.2 c.10 refers to the tenth canon of *Quaestio* 2 in *Causa* 12. A subdivision of the *causae* dealing with the sacrament of penance (*De Poenitentia*) is cited as *De Poen.* The other volumes of the *Corpus Iuris Canonici* were all divided into books which were subdivided into titles. Thus, X. 3.12.1 refers to the first canon of Title 12 in Book 3 of the Gregorian Decretals.

II. OTHER SOURCES

Bernardus Parmensis, *Gl. Ord.*	*Glossa Ordinaria* to the Gregorian Decretals in *Decretales Gregorii Papae IX* (Paris, 1601)
Dominicus de Sancto Gemignano, *Commentaria*	*Dominici de Sancto Geminiano Commentaria in Decretum* (Venice, 1504)
Felinus Sandeus, *Commentaria*	*Commentaria . . . in V Libros Decretalium* (Venice, 1570)

Guido de Baysio, *Rosarium* — *Rosarium seu in Decretorum Volumen Commentaria* (Venice, 1570)

Henricus de Bohic, *Distinctiones* — *In Quinque Decretalium Libros Commentaria* (Venice, 1576)

Hostiensis, *Commentaria* — *In Primum . . . Sextum Decretalium Librum Commentaria* (Venice, 1581)

Innocent IV, *Commentaria* — *In V Libros Decretalium Commentaria* (Venice, 1570)

Joannes Andreae, *Gl. Ord. ad Clem.* — *Glossa Ordinaria* to the Clementines in *Clementis Papae Quinti Constitutiones* (Paris, 1601)

———, *Gl. Ord. ad Sext.* — *Glossa Ordinaria* to the *Liber Sextus* in *Liber Sextus Decretalium Bonifacii Papae VIII* (Paris, 1601)

———, *Novella* — *Novella super Decretalibus* (Venice, 1605)

Joannes Monachus, *Glosa Aurea* — *Glosa Aurea super Sexto Decretalium Libro* (Paris, 1535)

Joannes Teutonicus, *Gl. Ord.* — *Glossa Ordinaria* to the *Decretum* in *Decretum Gratiani* (Paris, 1601)

Joannes de Turrecremata, *Repertorium* — *Repertorium Joannis de Turrecremata super Toto Decreto* (Lyons, 1519)

Lyndwood, *Provinciale* — *Provinciale (seu Constitutiones Angliae) continens constitutiones provinciales quatuordecim archiepiscoporum Cantuariensum . . . Cui adjiciuntur Constitutiones legatinae d. Othonis et d. Othoboni cum profundissimis annotationibus Johannis de Athona* (Oxford, 1679)

MS F.XI.605 — MS XI.605 of Sankt Florian, Stiftsbibliothek

MS Pal.Lat.658 — MS Pal.Lat.658 of the Biblioteca Vaticana

MS R.743 — MS 743 of the Bibliothèque municipale, Rouen

Panormitanus, *Commentaria* — *Abbati Panormitani omnia quae extant Commentaria* (Venice, 1588)

Raymundus, *Summa Iuris* — San Raymundo de Penyafort, *Summa Iuris*, ed. J. R. Serra (Barcelona, 1945)

Reg. Bronscombe — *The Registers of Walter Bronscombe (1257–80) and Peter Quivil (1280–91), Bishops of Exeter*, ed. F. C. Hingeston-Randolph (London, 1889)

Reg. Cantilupe — *Registrum Thome de Cantilupo Episcopi Herefordensis (1275–82)*, ed. R. G. Griffiths and W. W. Capes (Canterbury and York Soc., 1907)

Reg. Gandavo — *Registrum Simonis de Gandavo Episcopi Sarisbiriensis (1297–1315)*, ed. C. T. Flower and M. C. B. Dawes (Canterbury and York Soc., 1914–1934)

Reg. Grandisson	*The Register of John de Grandisson (1327–69), Bishop of Exeter*, ed. F. C. Hingeston-Randolph (London, 1894)
Reg. Kellawe	*The Register of Richard de Kellawe*, ed. T. D. Hardy (Rolls Series, 1875–1878)
Reg. Newport	*Registrum Radulphi Baldock, Gilberti Segrave, Ricardi Newport, et Stephani Gravesend*, ed. R. C. Fowler (Canterbury and York Soc., 1911)
Reg. Orleton	*Registrum Ade de Orleton Episcopi Herefordensis (1317–1327)*, ed. A. T. Bannister (Canterbury and York Soc., 1908)
Reg. Peckham	*Registrum Epistolarum Johannis Peckham Archiepiscopi Cantuariensis*, ed. C. T. Martin (Rolls Series, 1882–1886)
Reg. Quivil	See *Reg. Bronscombe*
Reg. Romeyn	*The Register of John le Romeyn, Lord Archbishop of York (1286–96)*, ed. W. Brown (Surtees Soc., 1913–1917)
Reg. Stapledon	*The Register of Walter Stapledon (1307–26), Bishop of Exeter*, ed. F. C. Hingeston-Randolph (London, 1892)
Reg. Swinfield	*Registrum Ricardi de Swinfield Episcopi Herefordensis (1283–1317)*, ed. W. W. Capes (Canterbury and York Soc., 1909)
Reg. Wickwane	*Register of William Wickwane, Lord Archbishop of York (1279–85)*, ed. W. Brown (Surtees Soc., 1907)
Reg. Winchelsey	*Registrum Roberti Winchelsey Archiepiscopi Cantuariensis (1294–1313)*, ed. Rose Graham (Canterbury and York Soc., 1917–1952)
Repetitiones	*Repetitionum in universas fere Iuris Canonici partes . . . volumina sex* (Venice, 1587)
Rufinus, *Summa*	*Die Summa Decretorum des Magister Rufinus*, ed. H. Singer (Paderborn, 1902)
Stephanus, *Summa*	*Die Summa des Stephanus Tornacensis*, ed. J. F. von Schulte (Giessen, 1891)
Summa Parisiensis	*The Summa Parisiensis on the Decretum Gratiani*, ed. T. P. McLaughlin (Toronto, 1952)
Wilkins	*Concilia Magnae Britanniae et Hiberniae*, ed. David Wilkins (4 vols.; London, 1737)

III. MODERN WORKS

Ashley, *Economic History*	W. J. Ashley, *An Introduction to English Economic History and Theory* (4th ed.; London, 1925)
Coulton, *Five Centuries*	G. G. Coulton, *Five Centuries of Religion* (4 vols.; Cambridge, 1923–1950)
Gasquet, *Parish Life*	F. A. Gasquet, *Parish Life in Mediaeval England* (New York, 1906)
Hartridge, *Vicarages*	R. A. R. Hartridge, *A History of Vicarages in the Middle Ages* (Cambridge, 1930)
Webb, *Poor Law History*, I, II	Sidney and Beatrice Webb, *English Local Government. English Poor Law History: Part I. The Old Poor Law* (London, 1927); *Part II. The Last Hundred Years* (2 vols.; London, 1929)

Notes

CHAPTER I: *Poverty* (Pages 1–21)

[1] Brian L. Woodcock, *Medieval Ecclesiastical Courts in the Diocese of Canterbury* (London, 1952), p. 80.

[2] *Roman Canon Law in the Church of England* (London, 1898), p. 100.

[3] A study of the teachings of the medieval Roman lawyers and an investigation of local manorial customs would also be of value. The canonistic works, however, constitute by far the most important legal sources for a study of this kind. Unlike the records of medieval Roman law and customary law they present at once an elaborately developed system of academic jurisprudence and the practically enforced law of a living society.

[4] Especially valuable are Georg Ratzinger, *Geschichte der kirchlichen Armenpflege* (2d ed.; Freiburg-im-Breisgau, 1884); G. G. W. Uhlhorn, *Die Christliche Liebestatigkeit in der alten Kirche* (3 vols.; Stuttgart, 1882–1890); Leon Lallemand, *Histoire de la Charité* (3 vols.; Paris, 1902–1912); W. Liese, *Geschichte der Caritas* (2 vols.; Freiburg-im-Breisgau, 1922). The best treatments of poor relief in medieval England are R. M. Clay, *The Medieval Hospitals of England* (London, 1909); W. J. Ashley, *An Introduction to English Economic History and Theory* (4th ed.; London, 1925), pp. 305–376; Sidney and Beatrice Webb, *English Local Government. English Poor Law History: Part I. The Old Poor Law* (London, 1927). E. M. Leonard, *Early History of English Poor Relief* (Cambridge, 1900), is good for the Tudor and Stuart periods but has only a few perfunctory pages on the Middle Ages.

[5] A sketch of the growth of the *Corpus Iuris Canonici* is given in R. C. Mortimer, *Western Canon Law* (Berkeley and Los Angeles, 1953), pp. 40–55. For a more detailed outline see P. Torquebiau and G. Mollat in *Dictionnaire de Droit Canonique*, s.v. *Corpus Iuris Canonici*. The volumes of the *Dictionnaire* which have so far appeared contain articles on most of the canonists mentioned in the text. The best guides to the bibliography on canonistic works are A. Van Hove,

Prolegomena ad Codicem Iuris Canonici. Commentarium Lovaniense in Codicem Iuris Canonici, I, i (Malines-Rome, 1945); and S. Kuttner, *Repertorium der Kanonistik* (Vatican City, 1937).

[6] The *Glossa Ordinaria* to the *Decretum* was written (1215–1217) by Joannes Teutonicus. Bernardus Parmensis produced a first version of his *Glossa Ordinaria* to the Gregorian Decretals in about 1241 and continued to make revisions in it down to the time of his death in 1266. The glosses on the *Liber Sextus* and the Clementines were the work of Joannes Andreae (in 1294–1303 and in 1326), and the gloss on the *Extravagantes Joannis XXII* was done by Zenzellinus de Cassanis in 1325.

[7] Guido de Baysio, *Rosarium ad Dist.*1 ante c.1, fol. 3[ra].

[8] One comes upon observations like this: "The extent of the hospitality afforded by the [medieval] Church is evident from the different types of institutions maintained. . . . There were *xenodochia*, where the pilgrims were supported, *ptochotrophia*, where the poor were received, *gerontocomia* or hospices for the indigent aged, *orphanotrophia*, wherein the orphans were cared for, and *brephotrophia*, where the infants of the poor received food." The author supports this by a reference to the *Glossa Ordinaria* on a canon of the *Decretum*. But the canon in question, which mentioned all these institutions, dated back to the fourth century, and Joannes Teutonicus, writing in the thirteenth century, was merely showing off his erudition by explaining what all these quaint old-fashioned terms meant. (*Gl. Ord. ad* C.23 q.8 c.23.) Certainly there were many hospitals and almshouses in the Middle Ages, but this text provides no real evidence as to how they were organized in the thirteenth century. As a more critical modern author observes: "Certains canonistes, plongés dans leur livres, paraissent au XIIIe siècle n'avoir connu les hôpitaux que dans les oeuvres de Justinien. . . ." Jean Imbert, *Les Hôpitaux en Droit Canonique* (Paris, 1947), p. 115 n. 1.

[9] *Opuscula Sancti Patris Francisci* (Quaracchi, 1904), p. 79. Again, in the twelfth-century life of St. Ailred of Rievaulx, the poverty of the early Cistercians was praised in these terms: "They venerate poverty, not the penury of the idle and negligent, but a poverty directed by a necessity of the will and sustained by the thoroughness of faith, and approved by divine love." *The Life of Ailred of Rievaulx*, trans. F. M. Powicke (London, 1950), p. 11.

[10] Cited by Guido de Baysio, *Rosarium ad* C.1 q.2 c.9, fol. 125[vb]: "Nota quod quidam sunt quos nativitas pauperes fecit, quam tamen paupertatem divino intuitu voluntarie patiuntur; alii sunt pauperes qui divino intuitu sive amore seipsos Christi pauperibus coniunxerunt ut Apostoli, qui relictis omnibus secuti sunt Christum . . . paupertas istorum voluntaria dicitur. Sunt alii pauperes sola cupiditatis habendae voracitate . . . istorum paupertas dicitur necessaria secundum Hu[guccio]."

[11] Webb, *Poor Law History*, II, ii, 992–994.

[12] *Gl. Ord. ad Sext.* 1.3.11.

[13] C.15 q.1 c.6.

[14] *Gl. Ord. ad* C.2 q.1 c.14.

[15] X. 1.32.1.

[16] *Dist.*86 c.26; *Dist.*88 c.1; C.5 q.3 c.3; X. 3.50.1.

[17] X. 2.20.8.

[18] *Gl. Ord. ad* X. 2.20.8: "Sed quare remittit ad ipsos quia licet sint pauperes

bene possunt venire. Potest dici quod ideo quia tales sunt quod non decet eos venire ad iudicem, forsitan quia nobilis et ita verecundatur venire propter nimiam paupertatem, licet tamen iste pauper alias honesta persona est."

[19] Hostiensis, *Commentaria ad* X. 2.20.8, fol. 86rb: "Hoc intelligi potest quando licet pauper sit tamen nobilis et honestus est et verecundatur venire propter paupertatem nimiam. . . . Vel dic hoc debere intelligi non de paupertate testis, sed principalis ipsum producere volentis . . . ideo in hoc casu mitti debet ad testes recipiendos et parcendum est paupertati. . . ."

[20] E.g., Gulielmus Durandus, Antonius de Butrio, Panormitanus. Their views were quoted by Felinus Sandeus in his *Commentaria ad* X. 2.20.8.

[21] *Rosarium ad* C.11 q.3 c.72, fols. 219vb–220ra.

[22] *Dist.*84 *ante* c.1.

[23] The various passages, in the order mentioned, are in the *Gl. Ord. ad* C.24 q.3 c.21, *Dist.*87 c.1, *Dist.*87 c.3, *Dist.*87 c.6 C.23 q.5 c.23. Much the same ambiguity existed in Roman law. B. Biondi has pointed out that Roman law imposed on clerics the duty of relieving the poor as a legal obligation, and also acknowledged the duty of state officials to give relief: "Adiuvare pauperes et in necessitatibus positos." *Ius*, 3 (1952), 233–239.

[24] X. 1.29.38.

[25] X. 2.2.15.

[26] Bernardus insisted that cases of "wretched persons" belonged in the first place to the secular courts, and that ecclesiastical courts could take cognizance of them only if the appropriate secular judge had refused to do justice. Following closely the text of the Decretals, he conceded an exception to this rule only when it was a case of enforcing immediate restitution of something seized by violence. See *Gl. Ord. ad* X. 1.29.38, 2.2.11, 3.39.4, 5.40.26.

[27] Innocent IV, *Commentaria ad* X. 1.29.38, p. 172: "Nota viduas non esse de foro ecclesiae . . . nisi quantum ad hoc, quod propriis iudicibus non facientibus eius iustitiae complementum ecclesiasticus iudex faciet. . . . Sed si viduae essent pauperes sicut ceteri pauperes etiam non negligentibus dominis vel iudicibus suis non tantum de oppressione eorum sed etiam de aliorum iuribus possunt conqueri ecclesiae . . . pupillorum autem et orphanorum causas audiet ecclesia, negligente iudice seculari ei facere iustitiam, etiam si sint divites, sicut de viduis diximus. . . . Idem in senibus. . . . Idem in cecis et mutilatis membris et leprosis et captivis et debilibus et diutino morbo fatigatis . . . nam miserabiles personae sunt. Pro maiori autem parte praedictae personae si sint divites coguntur sub iudicibus suis ordinariis respondere, si volunt sibi facere iustitiae complementum. . . . Sed objicies, quid est speciale in miserabilibus personis? . . . Respondeo, horum simplicem querimoniam aliquando ecclesia audit etiam non requisitis dominis, et semper audit quando priores domini renuunt eis facere iustitiam, nec dicitur eis, ite ad alium proximum superiorem. Sed in aliis non intromitteret se ecclesia quousque aliquem superiorem habet ad quem recurrere possit. . . . Item dicimus quod etiam praedictae personae si habito respectu ad ea quae possident sint pauperes, sed magnas hereditates vel castra petant, non venient ad ecclesiasticum iudicem, nisi prius deficiat secularis, quia causa cessat pro qua toleratum est quod iudex ecclesiasticus cognoscat etiam non negligente seculari scilicet quia de modica re agit." Innocent elsewhere maintained that by right the pope had jurisdiction over all cases of widows and that he conceded jurisdiction to secular courts in some

cases merely as an act of grace. *Commentaria ad* X. 2.2.11, p. 239. Hostiensis seems to have hesitated between the views of Bernardus Parmensis and those of Innocent IV. See his *Commentaria ad* X. 1.29.38, fol. 160ra; 2.2.8, fol. 11vb; 2.2.11, fol. 21ra; 2.2.15, fol. 15ra. His final comment, *Commentaria ad* X. 5.40.26, fol. 131ra, preserved Innocent's essential distinction. At this point Hostiensis wrote that cases of widows and other *miserabiles personae* belonged to the church courts when the party involved was genuinely powerless and wretched, or oppressed and unable to find justice elsewhere—otherwise not.

[28] Webb, *Poor Law History*, II, i, 249.

[29] X. 5.5.1. For a translation of the whole canon and the full text see H. J. Schroeder, *Disciplinary Decrees of the General Councils* (St. Louis, 1937), pp. 229, 556.

[30] X. 5.5.4; Schroeder, *op. cit.*, pp. 252, 567.

[31] *Gl. Ord. ad Dist.*37, c.12, and *additio* of Bartholomaeus Brixiensis to this gloss.

[32] Joannes Teutonicus, cited by Bernardus Parmensis, *Gl. Ord. ad* X. 5.5.4. This whole subject has recently been examined in detail by Gaines Post, Kimon Giocarinis, and Richard Kay, "The Medieval Heritage of a Humanistic Ideal: 'Scientia donum dei est, unde vendi non potest,' " *Traditio*, XI (1955), 195–234. The texts cited above and others bearing on this same point are printed in this article.

CHAPTER II: *Property* (Pages 22–44)

[1] Reinhold Niebuhr, *The Contribution of Religion to Social Work* (New York, 1932), p. 6; see also pp. 18–24.

[2] Marshall Baldwin, *The Mediaeval Church* (Ithaca, 1953), p. 3.

[3] Mary Richmond, *The Long View* (New York, 1930), p. 518.

[4] In the evaluation of such measures it is important to bear in mind that the economic context itself set limits to what could be achieved, especially in years of general dearth. The occasional season of crop failure and famine in the Middle Ages might be compared to the years of industrial depression and unemployment in the twentieth century. All systems of poor relief have proved inadequate to cope with the problems of mass unemployment. And that is not a criticism of the poor laws; mass unemployment is not a problem that can be dealt with by refinements of poor law, but only, if at all, by fiscal and monetary policy. Similarly, hunger arising from widespread crop failure was not a problem that could adequately have been dealt with by refinements of medieval poor law. The only eventual solution lay in the development of agricultural technology and communications.

[5] Acts 4:32–35.

[6] C.12 q.1 c.2.

[7] *Gl. Ord. ad* C.12 q.1 c.2.

[8] *Dist.*1 *ante* c.1. Gratian's views on natural law are discussed in A. J. Carlyle, *A History of Political Theory in the West* (London, 1928), II, 96–111, and a large number of canonistic texts on the subject are printed in O. Lottin, *Le droit naturel chez St. Thomas d'Aquin et ses prédécesseurs* (2d ed.; Bruges, 1931). In recent years there has grown up a substantial technical literature on the concept

of natural law in Gratian and the early decretists. The articles of Arnold, Composta, Delhaye, Giet, Leitmayer, Rota, Villey, and Wegner in the first three volumes of *Studia Gratiana* (Bologna, 1953–1955) deal with various facets of the problem and give references to other recent literature. (For this see especially page 440, note 8, in P. Delhaye, "Morale et droit canonique dans la 'Summa' d'Etienne de Tournai," *Studia Gratiana* (Bologna, 1953), I, 435–449.) It seems to me that much of the recent writing is overingenious in seeking to extract from the decretist works more elaborate and harmonious theories of natural law than the canonists themselves had actually devised. A particularly helpful introduction to the Roman law doctrines that inspired much of the canonistic reflection in this field is in E. Levy, "Natural Law in Roman Thought," *Studia et Documenta Historiae et Iuris*, 15 (1949), 1–23.

[9] *Dist.*1 c.7. Italics added.

[10] *Dist.*5 *ante* c.1. Gratian went on to explain that, although the universal rules of natural law were contained in the Old Testament, not everything in the Old Testament constituted natural law. The ceremonial observances prescribed for the Jews, for instance, applied only to that people at that time.

[11] *Dist.*8 c.1. St. Augustine, in this passage, was defending the action of the imperial authorities in confiscating the property of Donatist heretics. They could not claim their property by divine law, because by divine law all things were common. They could not claim it by human law, the law of the emperors, because it was precisely that law which dispossessed them.

[12] Stephanus Tornacensis, for instance, gave four meanings, then added, ". . . and if you do not shrink from yet another interpretation . . . ," and went on with a fifth. The canonist Honorius found as many as six meanings. S. Kuttner and E. Rathbone, "Anglo-Norman Canonists of the Twelfth Century," *Traditio*, VII (1949–1951), 355.

[13] When medieval thinkers referred to the primeval state of man, they commonly had in mind, of course, the condition of innocence before the Fall of Adam. But the canonists did not normally think of natural law as being essentially the law appropriate to that state. (By way of exception that view was put forward in the English *Summa Prima primi*, British Museum, Royal MS, 11.D.II, fol. 321[ra].) Gratian himself seems clearly to have conceived of natural law as a law known to man after the Fall but before the enactment of human codes of legislation.

[14] *Summa Parisiensis ad Dist.*8 c.1, p. 7.

[15] Rufinus, *Summa ad Dist.*1, p. 7: "Detractum autem ei [iuri naturali] est non utique in mandatis vel prohibitionibus, que derogationem nullam sentire queunt, sed in demonstrationibus—que scilicet natura non vetat non precipit, sed bona esse ostendit—et maxime in omnium una libertate et communi possessione; nunc enim iure civili hic est servus meus, ille est ager tuus." Likewise the English *Summa Omnis Qui Iuste* (*ca.* 1186), MS R.743, fol. 2[rb]. The French gloss, *Ecce Vicit Leo* (1202–1210), and the Bolognese *Glossa Palatina* (1210–1215) both used the argument that community of property in natural law was merely a *demonstratio* to explain the words attributed to St. Clement at C.12 q.2 c.10, MS F.XI.605, fol. 61[va], and MS Pal.Lat.658, fol. 49[rb].

[16] See the various texts presented in Lottin, *op. cit.*, and, for discussions on natural law and property among the later canonists, see Innocent IV, *Commentaria*

ad 3.34.8, p. 514; Hostiensis, *Commentaria ad* 3.34.8, fol. 128rb; Guido de Baysio, *Rosarium ad Dist.*1 c.1, fol. 3rb, *Dist.*1 c.7, fol. 4vb, C.12 q.1 c.2, fol. 223vb; Zenzellinus de Cassanis, *Gl. Ord. ad Extrav. Jo. XXII*, 1.14.4.

[17] Cited by Lottin, *op. cit.*, p. 110: "By natural law, that is, by rational judgment, all things are common, that is, to be shared in time of necessity with those in want. For natural reason leads us to approve that we should retain for ourselves only necessities and distribute what is left to our neighbors in need."

[18] *Gl. Ord. ad Dist.*1 c.7 (italics added). The same interpretation of the word "common" was presented in the gloss *Ecce Vicit Leo ad Dist.*1 c.7 and *ad* C.12 q.1 c.2, MS F.XI.605, fols. 2ra, 61va, and also in the *Glossa Palatina ad Dist.*47 c.8, MS Pal.Lat.658, fol. 12ra.

[19] *Gl. Ord. ad Dist.*1 c.7: "*Communis omnium*, i.e. nihil erat proprium alicui iure divino. Vel dic communis, i.e. communicanda tempore necessitatis ut 47 dist. *Sicut*, nam et secundum legem Rhod. tempore periculi cibaria maxime erant communia ut ff Ad leg. Rhod. l.2. *cum in eadem nave* in fine [Digest 14.2.2.2]."

[20] *Dist.*47 c.8.

[21] The text originally came from St. Basil and was in Greek. St. Ambrose made use of it in one of his homilies, but the precise form given by Gratian was a translation (with some interpolations) made by Rufinus of Aquileia (*ca.* 400). St. Basil's text is in Migne, *Patrologia Graeca*, 31, 261A–277C, that of St. Ambrose in Migne, *Patrologia Latina*, 17, 613–614, and that of Rufinus in *Patrologia Latina*, 21, 1741–1742. On this text see S. Giet, "La doctrine de l'appropriation des biens chez quelques-un des pères," *Recherches de Science Religieuse*, 35 (1948), 55–91, and "De trois textes de Gratien sur la propriété," *Studia Gratiana* (Bologna, 1954), II, 321–332.

[22] *Gl. Ord. ad Dist.*86 c.18: "*Possumus*, quod fit cum nobis necessaria subtrahimus, ad quod non tenemur . . . si autem hoc facimus commendandi sumus." See also *Gl. Ord. ad Dist.*47 c.8: "*Etiam violenter*, dicitur hic quod per violentiam dicitur auferre qui ultra necessaria sibi retinet . . . quod verum est si hoc fiat tempore necessitatis. . . ."

[23] "Finalmente rintracciata la fonte del famoso testo patristico: 'Pasce famem morientem. . . ,' " *Antonianum*, 27 (1952), 349–366; "Osservazioni critico-letterarie e dottrinale sul famoso testo 'Proprium nemo dicat . . .' e testi commessi," *Franciscan Studies*, 12 (1952), 214–231; *Determinatio superflui in doctrina Alexandri Halensis eiusque scholae* (Rome, 1953); "Le obbligazioni verso i poveri in un testo di S. Cesario reportata da Graziano (can.66. XVI, q.1) con falso attribuzione a S. Agostino," *Studia Gratiana* (Bologna, 1955), III, 51–81; "Estne obligatio iustitiae subvenire pauperibus?" *Apollinaris*, 29 (1956), 124–231; 30 (1957), 99–201. The comments in the text above are based mainly on this last study of Fr. Lio. See also O. Lottin, "La nature du devoir de l'aumône," *Psychologie et morale aux XIIe et XIIIe siècles*, III.ii (Louvain, 1949), pp. 299–313.

[24] *Rosarium ad Dist.*47 c.8, fol. 61vb. This follows precisely the teaching of St. Thomas in his *Commentum in Lib.IV Sententiarum*, D.15 q.2 a.1 q.4: ". . . it is commonly said that to give alms from superfluities is a matter of precept, and likewise to give alms to one who is in extreme need." St. Thomas explained that a state of "extreme need" existed when a man lacked even the bare essentials necessary to sustain life. Even a man without "superfluities" was obliged to help in such a case. That is to say, a man was bound to give up the comforts and amenities proper

to his station in life (which were not technically "superfluities") to save another from actual starvation. On the views of St. Thomas see L. Bouvier, *Le précepte de l'aumône chez saint Thomas d'Aquin* (Montreal, 1935). Guido de Baysio in another context wrote more tersely: "We are not bound to strip ourselves of necessities . . . but to give superfluities to the poor" (*Rosarium ad Dist.*86 c.14, fol. 101ᵛᵃ). In these discussions, the theologians and canonists were concerned to specify the bare minimum that had to be done as a matter of precept. To do more than the minimum was always commended as a meritorious act of charity.

²⁵ *Distinctiones ad* X. 5.38.4, p. 250.

²⁶ Lyndwood, *Provinciale*, p. 133, s.v. *Necessitati extremae:* "Et intelligo *necessitatem extremam,* non tantum in mortis articulo . . . sed etiam quando is qui necessitate patitur sustentari non potest. . . . Et praedicta intelligo vera, ut talis substentatio fiat de eo quod alicui, deductis necessariis pro sustentatione propria, et suorum, ac onerum sibi incumbentium, superest. Illud namque superfluum de necessitate praecepti est talem necessitatem patientibus erogandum . . . et quae apud nos reputari debent superflua judicare debemus, non considerando ad omnes causas quae contigere possent in futurum, sed ad ea quae probabiliter et in pluribus occurrunt. His quae dixi, concordat *Thomas* in scriptis super 4. di. 15, et addit, quod tunc intelligendus est casus extremae necessitatis, quando apparent signa probabilia extremae necessitatis futurae, nisi ei subveniatur. . . . Non enim expectanda est ultima necessitas, quia tunc forte non posset juvari natura jam fame vel siti consumpta."

²⁷ *Gl. Ord. ad Dist.*41 c.7.

²⁸ *Gl. Ord. ad Sext.* 3.16.1. The canonists commonly taught that a cleric was entitled to a standard of living appropriate to his "quality" or to his "nobility and learning." See, e.g., *Gl. Ord. ad* C.10 q.2 c.7; *Gl. Ord. ad* X. 1.3.17, 3.4.6; Innocent IV, *Commentaria ad* X. 1.3.17, p. 19; Hostiensis, *Commentaria ad* X. 1.3.17, fol. 15ᵛᵇ.

²⁹ *Dist.*86 c.21; *Gl. Ord. ad* C.12 q.1 c.11; *Gl. Ord. ad Dist.*86 c.19; *Dist.*42 ante c.1.

³⁰ Joannes Teutonicus, *Gl. Ord. ad* C.12 q.2 c.11: "Some say that a man ought rather to die than to steal. It is more humane to say that very great necessity excuses." Bernardus Parmensis, *Gl. Ord. ad* X. 5.18.3: "From the fact that penance is imposed [for a theft] it is gathered that the need was only slight, for if it had been great a penance would not have been imposed, . . . because in necessity all things are common." Bernardus went on to explain that no degree of want could justify a sin, but that theft in these circumstances was not a sin since the thief had a right to what he took. Similarly, Innocent IV, *Commentaria ad* X. 5.18.3, p. 615, and Hostiensis, *Commentaria ad* X. 5.18.3, fol. 55ʳ.

³¹ Lottin, "La nature du devoir de l'aumône," p. 312: "Il est d'abord certain que les théologiens n'entendaient point parler de justice légale ou sociale. . . ." Similarly Lio, *Apollinaris*, 30 (1957), 199.

³² *Gl. Ord. ad Dist.*47 c.8, s.v. *Aliena.*

³³ On the origins of the procedure of *denunciatio evangelica* see C. Lefebvre, "Contribution à l'étude des origines et du développement de la 'denunciatio evangelica' en droit canonique," *Ephemerides Iuris Canonici*, 6 (1950), 60–93, and for a more detailed discussion of this whole question see below, chap. vi. The comment of Joannes Teutonicus was at *Dist.*47 c.8: "Numquid ergo pauperes ipsum

148 NOTES

possunt petere? Non directo iudicio, sed denuntiare possunt ecclesiae illum qui non dat, et sic ecclesia potest eum cogere ut det." At another point in his gloss Joannes compared a pauper seeking alms with a man seeking a dispensation. Sometimes, he pointed out, a dispensation was due, and an ecclesiastical judge would sin if he refused to grant it. But if he did refuse there was no law by which the petitioner could bring suit. Joannes' solution here was the same as that when he explicitly considered the case of a poor man seeking alms: the petitioner should appeal to a superior by "imploring the office of the judge," that is, by the procedure of *denunciatio evangelica* (Gloss *ad* C.1 q.7 c.18).

³⁴ C.12 q.1 c.28; C.12 q.2 c.70; C.16 q.1 c.68.

³⁵ C.12 q.1 *post* c.24.

³⁶ *Gl. Ord. ad* C.12 q.1 *post* c.25, and *ad* C.1 q.2 c.6: "Si abundantes de bonis ecclesiae suscipiunt, sive absentes sive praesentes sunt, licet non debet eis denegari portio, quia nemo cogitur suis stipendiis militare, mortaliter tamen peccant, praesertim si ex cupiditate sua reservant."

³⁷ *Commentaria ad* X. 3.5.4, p. 425: "Tamen non credimus quod qui habet beneficium vivere debeat de patrimonio, sed de altari. . . ."

³⁸ Huguccio seems to have been the first of the decretists to anticipate the later view that ecclesiastical property belonged to the whole Christian community. *Summa ad* C.23 q.7 c.3: "These goods belong to the Catholic Church, not to the walls, but to the congregation of the faithful" (cited by P. Gillet, *La personnalité juridique en droit ecclésiastique* [Malines, 1927], p. 101). This text, however, was apparently overlooked by later canonists who commonly attributed to Huguccio the view that church property belonged simply to God. E.g., Bernardus Parmensis, *Gl. Ord. ad* X. 5.40.13; Hostiensis, *Commentaria ad* X. 5.40.13; Henricus de Bohic, *Distinctiones ad* X. 5.40.13.

³⁹ Gloss *Ecce Vicit Leo ad* C.12 q.1 c.13, MS F.XI.605, fols. 61ᵛᵇ–62ʳᵃ; *Glossa Palatina ad* C.12 q.1 c.13, MS Pal.Lat.658, fol. 49ᵛᵇ. These glosses are printed in my book, *Foundations of the Conciliar Theory* (Cambridge, 1955), pp. 118–119.

⁴⁰ *Gl. Ord. ad* C.12 q.1 c.13.

⁴¹ *Commentaria ad* X. 2.12.4, p. 267.

⁴² *Commentaria ad* X. 3.34.8, p. 515.

⁴³ *Commentaria ad* X. 2.12.4, fol. 42ᵛᵃ, and *ad* X. 3.34.8, fol. 128ᵛᵇ.

⁴⁴ *Distinctiones ad* X. 5.40.13, p. 300. Similarly Joannes Monachus, *Glosa Aurea ad Sext.* 3.9.2; Joannes Andreae, *Gl. Ord. ad Sext.* 3.9.2; Panormitanus, *Commentaria ad* X. 2.12.4, III, fol. 237ᵛᵃ; Dominicus de Sancto Gemignano, *Commentaria ad* C.12 q.1 c.13, fol. 192ʳᵇ⁻ᵛᵃ; Joannes de Turrecremata, *Repertorium ad* C.12 q.1 c.16, II, fols. 211ᵛᵇ–212ʳᵃ.

CHAPTER III: *Charity* (Pages 44–67)

¹ Mark 12:30–31; Luke 6:31; Luke 6:38; Rom. 12:5.

² Matt. 25:34–40.

³ X. 5.38.14.

⁴ See the introduction to his *Das Armenwesen und die Armengesetzgebung in Europäischen Staaten* (Berlin, 1870).

⁵ Franz Ehrle, *Beitrage zur Geschichte und Reform der Armenpflege* (Freiburg-im-Breisgau, 1881), pp. 18–24.

[6] Ashley, *Economic History*, Part II, p. 316. The work was first published in 1893.

[7] *Ibid.*, pp. 338, 331, 340.

[8] *Ibid.*, p. 330.

[9] *Ibid.*, pp. 330, 339, 317, 340.

[10] *Rosarium ad Dist.*47 c.8. Guido de Baysio was again following the teaching of St. Thomas.

[11] *Gl. Ord. ad Dist.*35 c.1.

[12] C.1 q.1 c.27; C.14 q.5 c.3; C.24 q.1 c.28.

[13] *Summa Parisiensis ad* C.14 q.5 *ante* c.1, p. 171.

[14] Stephanus, *Summa ad* C.1 q.1 c.27, p. 128.

[15] Joannes Teutonicus, *Gl. Ord. ad Dist.*90, c.2; Raymundus, *Summa Iuris*, X, 70; Bernardus Parmensis, *Gl. Ord. ad* X. 3.30.23, 5.40.13; Hostiensis, *Commentaria ad* X. 5.40.13.

[16] *Rosarium ad* C.1 q.1 c.27, fol. 115va.

[17] On this theme see especially A. Guillaume, *Jeune et charité dans l'église latine des origines au XIIe siècle* (Paris, 1954).

[18] Rufinus, *Summa ad Dist.*86 *post* c.5, p. 176.

[19] *Gl. Ord. ad* C.12 q.1 c.7, and *ad Dist.*86 c.18.

[20] *Commentaria ad* X. 3.24.1, fol. 69ra. The word he used was *rusticus*—a country bumpkin.

[21] *De Poen. Dist.*3 c.19.

[22] *Gl. Ord. ad De Poen. Dist.*3 c.19: "Non ergo se fallant qui per largas eleemosynas fructus vel pecuniae se existimant impunitatem emere, quia qui diligit iniquitatem odit animam suam, et qui odit animam suam non est ei Deus misericors sed crudelis."

[23] C.23 q.6 *post* c.4, *Dist.*86 c.14, *Dist.*45 c.13. Cf. E. F. Bruck, "Ethics vs. Law: St. Paul, the Fathers of the Church and the 'Cheerful Giver' in Roman Law," *Traditio*, 2 (1944), 97–121.

[24] *Gl. Ord. ad Dist.*45 c.13, and *Rosarium ad Dist.*45 c.13, fol. 59va.

[25] *Rosarium ad De Poen. Dist.*3 c.19, fol. 372vb. On the need for right intention see also *Gl. Ord. ad* C.1 q.1 c.65, C.23 q.6 *post* c.4; *Gl. Ord. ad* X. 4.1.20; Hostiensis, *Commentaria ad* X. 4.1.20, fol. 6vb; Henricus de Bohic, *Distinctiones ad* X. 5.38.4, p. 249.

[26] Webb, *Poor Law History*, I, 4–5. The relevant decretist texts are published and the whole question discussed in more detail than is possible here in my forthcoming article, "The Decretists and the 'Deserving Poor,'" in *Comparative Studies in Society and History*.

[27] The ones most commonly cited in favor of indiscriminate charity to all were *Dist.*42 c.2, *Dist.*86 c.21, C.1 q.2 c.2, C.11 q.3 c.103, C.16 q.1 c.5, C.23 q.4 c.35. And, on the other side, *Dist.*86 c.14, C.5 q.5 c.2, C.16 q.1 c.68, C.23 q.4 c.37.

[28] *Dist.*42 *post* c.1.

[29] *Dist.*42 c.2.

[30] *Dist.*86 *post* c.6. The distinction between "man" and "sinner" was taken from a passage of St. Augustine quoted at C.23 q.4 c.35.

[31] *Dist.*86 c.9.

[32] *Gl. Ord. ad Dist.*86 c.7.

[33] *Dist.*86 cc.14,16,17.

[34] *Gl. Ord. ad Dist.*42 c.2.

[85] *Gl. Ord. ad Dist.*86 c.16; *Gl. Ord. ad* X. 3.2.1; Hostiensis, *Commentaria ad* X. 3.2.1, fol. 5[rb]. The qualification was always made that the relative had to be genuinely in a state of need.

[86] See U. Nicolini, "Il trattato 'De Alimentis' di Martino da Fano," *Atti de Congresso Internazionale di Diritto Romano e di Storia del Diritto* (Milan, 1951), pp. 339–371. The work was based mainly on Roman law sources, but much of it was included in the canonistic *Speculum Iudiciale* of Gulielmus Durandus.

[37] *Gl. Ord. ad Dist.*86 c.14, and *ad Dist.*30 c.1: "Sed pone quod habes patrem haereticum. Numquid preferes ipsum extraneo bono. Petrus Manducator dixit hanc quaestionem esse nebulam et tenebrosam aquam in nubibus aeris. Sed dicas quod patrem, qualiscunque sit, debemus praeponere extraneo, etiam sancto in his quae spectant ad opus misericordiae in providendo ei in necessariis, nisi alter magis indigeat, quia tunc potius tenemur extraneo subvenire." Joannes was following the opinion of Huguccio on this point. Similarly *Glossa Palatina ad Dist.*30 c.1, MS Pal.Lat.658, fol. 8[ra]; Raymundus, *Summa Iuris*, X, 70; Guido de Baysio, *Rosarium ad Dist.*86 c.14, fol. 101[rb].

[38] C.5 q.5 c.2, and, again, C.23 q.4 c.37.

[39] *Gl. Ord. ad Dist.*82 *ante* c.1: "Ei qui potest laborare, non debet ecclesia providere. Integritas enim et robur membrorum in conferenda eleemosyna est attendenda, C. *De mendi. val.* l.1 lib.11 [Code, 11.26.1], quia robusti de cibo securi sine labore frequenter iustitiam negligunt. . . ." The same view was put forward in the *Glossa Palatina* and in the gloss *Ecce Vicit Leo*, MS Pal.Lat.658, fol. 20[ra], and MS F.XI.605, fol. 25[va].

[40] *Gl. Ord. ad Dist.*86 c.19. See also C.1 q.2 cc.5,7.

[41] Rufinus, *Summa ad Dist.*42 *ante* c.1, pp. 100–101.

[42] *Summa Iuris*, X, 70.

[43] *Gl. Ord. ad Dist.*42 c.2: "If anyone asks for food it is to be given to all indifferently, . . . unless a man, being sure of his food, may neglect justice, because then it is to be taken from him unless he is already dying of hunger. . . . But if we have not enough for all, then we should give rather to the good than the evil, to a relative rather than a stranger." Again the comments of the *Glossa Palatina* and the gloss *Ecce Vicit Leo* on *Dist.*42 c.2 presented substantially the same doctrine (MS Pal.Lat.658, fol. 10[vb], and MS F.XI.605, fol. 18[rb–va]). The English *Summa Omnis Qui Iuste* had a particularly elaborate discussion of the problem. After reviewing at length various earlier opinions, the author continued with a series of distinctions. Either the man who sought alms sought them as a due stipend, claiming to be a priest, in which event he was to be examined; or he simply asked for charity. In that event he was either unknown or known. If unknown he was to be helped. If known he was either worthy or unworthy (*honestus* or *inhonestus*). If he was *inhonestus* nothing was to be given unless he was actually starving. If he was *honestus*, but not really in need, nothing was to be given again: "To give to him is nothing but wasting." If he really was in need then the resources of the one from whom he sought help had to be considered: "If a man has nothing good intention suffices. . . . If he has moderate means he shall do what he can. . . . If he has ample means he shall distribute charity in due order. . . . If he has enough for all he owes to all . . . lest he be judged a thief." (MS R.743, fol. 19[vb].)

[44] *Distinctiones ad* X. 5.38.14, p. 249: ". . . aut quaeris de pauperibus in ex-

trema necessitate constitutis et illis fieri debeat [eleemosina] de necessitate precepti.
. . . Aut de aliis quam de ribaldis quotidie ludentibus ad asardum, et illis fieri
potest et debet ut hic. Distinctione tamen habita inter illos qui petunt eleemosynam
ex debito ut praedicatorum. . . . Et illos qui petunt pro sustentatione corporis,
quo casu si potest omnibus sufficere, omnibus dare debes. . . . Si non potes omnibus
sufficere, tunc dicit Ambrosius novem esse consideranda, scilicet, causam, fidem,
locum, tempus, modum, necessitatem, sive sanguinis propinquitatem, debilitatem,
aetatem, conditionem sive nobilitatem. . . . Aut quaeris de illis ribaldis qui ludunt
quotidie ad asardum, et talibus non debemus facere eleemosinam. . . ."
    [45] X. 1.4.10, X. 2.28.53, X. 3.5.23.
    [46] This point was much argued. The most important texts were C.1 q.2 c.2,
which argued against conversion of infidels by bribes, and C.11 q.2 c.103, a decree
by Pope Gregory VII: "If anyone wishes to give to excommunicates, not to sustain
their pride, but for the sake of humanity, we do not forbid it."
    [47] *Rosarium ad Dist*.42 c.2, fol. 54[vb].
    [48] *Gl. Ord. ad* C.13 q.2 c.19. Joannes was commenting here specifically on an-
other form of medieval charity, the offering of prayers for the souls of the dead.
But to illustrate his general principle, "It is better to do too much than to do nothing
at all," he referred to *Dist*.42 c.2 (St. John Chrysostom's text on indiscriminate
almsgiving).
    [49] F. M. Page, "The Customary Poor Law of Three Cambridgeshire Manors,"
Cambridge Historical Journal, 3 (1929–1931), 125–133. The quotation is on
page 133. Further evidence concerning provision for the poor in manorial law has
been collected by Fr. J. A. Raftis, and will be presented in his forthcoming study
on the estates of Ramsey Abbey.

CHAPTER IV: *Institutions* (Pages 67–89)

    [1] *Dist*.82 *ante* c.1, *Dist*.87 *ante* c.1, *Dist*.84 *ante* c.1, *Dist*.85 *ante* c.1.
    [2] *Gl. Ord. ad Dist*.82 c.1.
    [3] Gratian introduced the subject by explaining that a bishop should be generous
(*liberalis*) to those in need. All through this section of the *Decretum* he had been
following closely an early collection of canons known as the Canons of the Apostles.
The Canons of the Apostles did mention hospitality as necessary in a bishop, but
they did not refer specifically to the virtue of *liberalitas*. The canonists, therefore,
sometimes asked why Gratian had departed from his model at this point, and the
answer given was that the chapters on *liberalitas* were simply a continuation of the
discussion on hospitality which Gratian had begun in the previous *Distinctio*. Thus,
Rufinus wrote, "What is said here about hospitality relates to the earlier chapter
declaring that it behooves a bishop to be hospitable. For, if he refuses to open his
hand to petitioners, how is it to be supposed that he would care for those received
into his house?" (*Summa ad Dist*.86 *post* c.5, p. 175.) Similarly, Joannes Teutonicus, *Gl. Ord. ad Dist*.86 *post* c.5, and Guido de Baysio, *Rosarium ad Dist*.85
ante c.1, fol. 100[va]. On the other hand, the canonists occasionally distinguished between almsgiving and hospitality, using the latter word to mean only the feeding
and lodging of travelers. Thus, the author of the *Summa Omnis Qui Iuste* suggested
that St. John Chrysostom's exhortation to indiscriminate charity might refer only
to the reception of travelers, not to almsgiving in general: "Perhaps hospitality is
one thing, almsgiving another, because it is hard for a traveler to answer an investi-

gator." (*Summa ad Dist.*42 c.2, MS R.743, fol. 19vb.) Similarly, Stephanus Tornacensis, *Summa ad Dist.*42 c.2, p. 62, and, for a later example, William Lyndwood, cited on pages 121–122. Thus, the word hospitality could be used in two ways: in a broad sense to refer to the relief of need in general (the more common use among the canonists), or in a narrower sense to refer to the reception of travelers as distinct from other forms of charitable activity. It is usually clear enough from the context which sense is intended.

[4] Coulton, *Five Centuries*, III, 154–155.

[5] Coulton's one specific example of such a distortion, which he attributes to Joannes Teutonicus in his *Glossa Ordinaria*, seems to be based on a misunderstanding of the canonists' way of using cross references. See *Five Centuries*, III, 204.

[6] C.12 q.1 c.23.

[7] C.12 q.2 c.23 and cc.26–31. The earliest text cited is attributed to Pope Simplicius (468–483). Others are taken from Pope Gelasius I (492–496) and Pope Gregory I (590–604).

[8] The most recent detailed study on the complicated history of the tithing system is that of C. Boyd, *Tithes and Parishes in Medieval Italy* (Ithaca, 1952). Although concerned especially with conditions in Italy, it provides information on the growth of the general law of tithes. On the doctrine of Gratian in particular, see E. Melicher, "Der Zehent als Kirchensteuer bei Gratian," *Studia Gratiana*, II (Bologna, 1954), pp. 387–407. The author concludes that "since the breakdown of the Roman Empire, Gratian was the first man to produce a comprehensive theory of taxes of a public character." A good sketch of the development of the parishes themselves is that of G. W. O. Addleshaw, *The Development of the Parochial System from Charlemagne to Urban II* (York, 1954). I have not been able to see a second pamphlet by the same author, *Rectors, Vicars and Patrons in 12th and early 13th Century Canon Law* (York, 1956).

[9] A good brief account of the development of the system of patronage and its relation to the practice of appropriation is in Hartridge, *Vicarages*, pp. 1–22. There is a complex literature on the growth of the "proprietary church system." Hartridge's pages refer to the work of Ulrich Stutz and other major authorities.

[10] In actual practice, in England, there seems to have been virtually no alienation of tithes to laymen in the high Middle Ages. The abuse was much more prevalent on the Continent.

[11] Ashley, *Economic History*, Part II, p. 309; Coulton, *Five Centuries*, III, 198–214; Webb, *Poor Law History*, I, 3.

[12] Medieval lawyers and administrators seldom sought to specify an arithmetical proportion of parish revenues to be spent on the poor. When they did so, their figures bore little relation to the classical fourfold division. In different contexts I have come upon the following proportions suggested as reasonable for the poor: a half, a quarter, a fifth, a sixth, an eighth, and a tenth. See pages 78–79, 100, 122.

[13] C.12 q.1 *post* c.25 and *post* c.27.

[14] *Summa Parisiensis ad* C.12 q.1 *post* c.25 and *post* c.27, p. 158.

[15] *Gl. Ord. ad* C.12 q.1 *post* c.27, C.12 q.2 c.23.

[16] Lyndwood, *Provinciale*, p. 132.

[17] The phrase comes originally from St. Paul, I Tim. 6:8. It was cited in the *Decretum* at C.12 q.1 c.7, and was often repeated by the canonists; e.g., *Gl. Ord.*

ad C.10 q.2 c.7, C.16 q.1 c.68; *Gl. Ord. ad* X. 2.26.2, 3.26.9; Hostiensis, *Commentaria ad* X. 3.26.9, fol. 75va.

[18] C.12 q.1 c.68. See, e.g., *Gl. Ord. ad* X. 2.26.2, 3.5.12; Hostiensis, *Commentaria ad* X. 2.26.2, fol. 148rb, 3.5.12, fol. 17rb, 3.13.2, fol. 52ra; Henricus de Bohic, *Distinctiones ad* X. 3.17.1, p. 430.

[19] See chap. ii, n. 28. Coulton, *Five Centuries*, III, 199, and, following him, Hartridge, *Vicarages*, p. 36, complain that the English canonist, John of Ayton, taught that a parish priest was entitled to nothing but food and clothes. But, again, the words must be understood against the general background of canonistic teaching on the point.

[20] *Gl. Ord. ad* X. 3.26.9, 3.1.9, 1.3.17. "Debet enim talis esse quae sufficiat sibi et suis . . . et quod adveniens possit recipere, et iura episcopalia persolvere."

[21] *Gl. Ord. ad* X. 3.4.6, 3.5.12, 3.5.30, 3.5.33, 3.7.1, and *ad Sext.* 1.16.19, 3.4.1.

[22] *Gl. Ord. ad Extrav. Jo. XXII*, 1.3.1. Similarly Hostiensis, *Commentaria ad* X. 3.17.1, fol. 57va, and Henricus de Bohic, *Distinctiones ad* X. 3.17.1, p. 430. Zenzellinus was commenting on a decree which used the phrase *hospitalitas debita* —due hospitality: "Per hoc autem quod dicit, debita, videtur innuere quod necessitatis, non tantum voluntatis est hospitalitas, et in beneficiatis hoc certum est. . . . Sed quid de aliis, puta laicis et clericis non beneficiatis, est ne quo ad eos necessitatis? Ber[nardus Parmensis] innuere videtur quod sic, intantum quod excommunicari possint, nisi hospites recipiant . . . *de empt. et vend.* c.1 [X. 3.17.1]. Inno[cent] tamen contrarium ibi notat. Host[iensis] autem videtur applaudere opinioni Ber. dicens quod non sufficit solvere integram decimam nisi de novem partibus eis remanentibus eleemosynam faciant. . . . Tu potes dicere quod illi in foro contentioso non dicuntur adstricti ad hospitalitatem, cum per legem nullus benefacere sit cogendus, cum coactus nullum meritum consequeretur. Sed in foro animae secus dicas. . . ." Zenzellinus seems here to overlook the fact that, according to canonistic teaching, to give alms was not always an act of pure benevolence, but sometimes an act of simple justice, and that to withhold alms was sometimes an act of willful injustice. This was pointed out by later canonists who considered the question. See chapter vi for a more detailed discussion on the point.

[23] Joannes Teutonicus, *Gl. Ord. ad* C.16 q.1 c.68; Innocent IV, *Commentaria ad* X. 3.5.12, p. 427; Hostiensis, *Commentaria ad* X. 3.5.12, fol. 17rb; Zenzellinus de Cassanis, *Gl. Ord. ad Extrav. Jo. XXII*, 1.3.1.

[24] *Wilkins*, II, 57.

[25] Petrus de Ancharano, *Commentaria ad* X. 3.5.12; Panormitanus, *Commentaria ad* X. 1.3.17, I, 150, and *ad* X. 3.5.12, VI, fol. 43vb; Lyndwood, *Provinciale*, p. 133.

[26] A. Savine, *English Monasteries on the Eve of the Dissolution* (Oxford, 1909).

[27] R. H. Snape, *English Monastic Finances in the Later Middle Ages* (Cambridge, 1926), pp. 110–118. The editor of the Norwich rolls estimated that "clear and doubtful" charitable expenditures amounted to 10.8 per cent of total receipts (but this included expenses of hospitality to wealthy visitors). H. W. Saunders, *An Introduction to the Rolls of Norwich Cathedral Priory* (Norwich, 1930), pp. 121–127, 169–171. Hartridge was very critical of the monasteries' poor relief efforts (*Vicarages*, pp. 155 ff.). F. A. Gasquet, at the other extreme, took a very favorable view in his *English Monastic Life* (London, 1904). A more moderate

discussion of the question is that of G. Baskerville, *English Monks and the Suppression of the Monasteries* (London, 1937), pp. 25–32.

[28] Claude Jenkins, "The Register of Archbishop Odo Rigaldi of Rouen," *Church Quarterly Review*, 101 (1925). The difficulties of arriving at any final truth in this matter are well illustrated by the case of the Abbey of Beaulieu. In 1235 this abbey secured the appropriation of the parish of St. Keverne, claiming in the usual way that it needed additional income to meet the expenses of hospitality. But the rector of the parish wrote a letter protesting that the abbey was in an unfrequented place where there was no need to provide hospitality, and that in fact it received hardly any guests at all. (*Victoria County History, Hampshire*, II, 141 ff., and Hartridge, *Vicarages*, p. 224.) This seems to provide firsthand contemporary evidence of the worst kind of abuse. But when, quite recently, a thirteenth-century account book of Beaulieu was analyzed, it was found that the expenses of hospitality in this monastery were indeed very heavy. See C. H. Talbot, "A Cistercian Account Book," *The Listener*, 55 (1955), 178: "In the year for which we have accounts the hospice spent nearly £120 in entertaining guests of one kind or another, nearly six times as much as the expenses of the secular infirmary. The poor at the gate were evidently a permanent feature of the place and it was the duty of the porter to care for them. Three times a week he distributed the bread remaining over from the refectory, the infirmary, the abbot's table and other offices, and every night of the year thirteen of them were to receive lodging, whilst at Christmas and other great feasts their number was to equal that of the monks in the community. . . . Only during the time of harvest was this hospitality restricted, for then it was given only to travellers, pilgrims, the very old and young, and the sick. Those who could work had to earn their bread."

[29] Eric St. John Brooks, ed., *The Irish Cartularies of Llanthony Prima and Secunda* (Dublin, 1953), pp. 276–277. The papal decision confirmed the rights of the priory; but vicarages assessed by the bishop were to be established in the parishes in question, and the priory undertook to make an annual payment of forty marks to the bishop.

[30] Canon 9. For the text of this canon, and a translation, see H. J. Schroeder, *Disciplinary Decrees of the General Councils* (St. Louis, 1937), pp. 222, 553.

[31] Canon 17; Schroeder, *op. cit.*, pp. 228, 555. This decree was included in the Gregorian Decretals at 1.38.3. It was reinforced by a decree of Pope Clement III, included in the Decretals at 1.10.2, which was specifically directed against abuses of monastic patrons. According to the pope, the patrons provided only hired priests instead of appointing permanent parsons to their parishes, men whom they could remove at will and who were so burdened with payments to the monks that they could not pay to the bishop the sums due from the parishes nor maintain proper hospitality. When that situation arose, the bishop was to act according to the decree of the Third Lateran Council and himself appoint a permanent parson to the church. Earlier, Pope Alexander III had written to the archdiocese of York in England forbidding the monks there to reduce the incomes of priests serving their churches without permission of the archbishop. This too was included in the Decretals (3.5.10).

[32] Canon 32; Schroeder, *op. cit.*, pp. 269, 573; included in the Decretals at 3.5.30.

[33] Bernardus Parmensis, *Gl. Ord. ad* X. 3.5.30.

[34] X. 3.5.12.

[35] *Sext.* 3.4.1.

[36] *Clem.* 3.12.1. A report of earlier canonistic discussion on this point, citing the views of Tancred, Goffredus de Trano, Innocent IV, Hostiensis, and Guido de Baysio, was given by Joannes Andreae in his *Gl. Ord. ad Clem.* 3.12.1.

[37] Jean Imbert, *Les hôpitaux en droit canonique* (Paris, 1947). Imbert presents a detailed study of the general canon law relating to hospitals, but is mainly concerned with French institutions. The only general survey of English medieval hospitals is the old book of Rotha Mary Clay, *The Medieval Hospitals of England* (London, 1909). Miss Clay is now working on a revision of this early work. On medieval German hospitals see S. Reicke, *Das Deutsche Spital und sein Recht im Mittelalter* (Stuttgart, 1932). A good general survey of hospital law from classical times down to the modern era is provided by E. Nasalli Rocca, *Il diritto ospedaliero nei suoi lineamenti storici* (Milan, 1956).

[38] For a list of English hospitals see D. Knowles and R. N. Hadcock, *Medieval Religious Houses* (London, 1953), pp. 250-324.

[39] *Clem.* 3.11.2. The decree was promulgated in the Council of Vienne. For text and translation see Schroeder, *op. cit.,* pp. 391, 613.

[40] Lapi de Castellione, *De Hospitalitate* in *Tractatus Universi Iuris* (Venice, 1584-1586), XIV, fols. 162-167.

[41] *De Hospitalitate,* fol. 162[vb].

[42] Panormitanus faced this question squarely when he restated the platitude that a cleric's income should be proportionate to his "nobility, dignity, and learning," and then asked: "Why should we have regard for such external qualities in divine matters?" He answered that it was because such qualities served the public good (*per has qualitates providetur bono universali*). *Commentaria ad X.* 1.3.17, I, 150.

[43] C. M. Fraser, ed., *Records of Antony Bek, Bishop and Patriarch,* Surtees Society, 162 (Durham and London, 1953), p. 6. The decree added that the dean of the new church should be responsible for maintaining hospitality.

[44] Henricus de Bohic, *Distinctiones ad X.* 5.9.15, p. 170.

CHAPTER V: *Theory and Practice* (Pages 89-109)

[1] Gasquet, *Parish Life,* p. 84.

[2] Ashley, *Economic History,* Part II, p. 310, citing *Canterbury Tales,* Prologue, ll. 488-492.

[3] *Early History of English Poor Relief* (Cambridge, 1900).

[4] Webb, *Poor Law History,* I, 3.

[5] See especially *Ten Medieval Studies* (3d ed.; Cambridge, 1930), pp. 162-163, and *Five Centuries,* III, 198-214, 650-654.

[6] Gasquet, *op. cit.,* pp. 16-17.

[7] On the efforts of English bishops to implement the reform decrees of the Fourth Lateran Council see M. Gibbs and J. Lang, *Bishops and Reform, 1215-1272* (Oxford, 1934). There are several general accounts of English church life in the Middle Ages less polemical in tone than those of Gasquet and Coulton: e.g., J. R. H. Moorman, *Church Life in England in the Thirteenth Century* (Cambridge, 1945); K. L. Wood-Legh, *Studies in Church Life in England under Edward III* (Cambridge, 1934); A. Hamilton Thompson, *The English Clergy and Their Organization in the Later Middle Ages* (Oxford, 1947).

[8] C. R. Cheney, *From Becket to Langton* (Manchester, 1956).

[9] Thorold Rogers, *Six Centuries of Work and Wages* (London, 1884), pp. 169–187. Details of wages paid to different grades of workmen in the building industry are given in L. F. Salzman, *Building in England* (Oxford, 1952), pp. 68–81. On the social background and standard of living of the parish clergy see H. G. Richardson, "The Parish Clergy of the Thirteenth and Fourteenth Centuries," *Transactions of the Royal Historical Society*, 3d series, VI (1912), 89–128.

[10] *Wilkins*, I, 587.

[11] Synodal Constitutions of Peter Quivil, Bishop of Exeter, *Wilkins*, II, 147.

[12] *Dist.*91 c.3. On the secular occupations of parish clergy in England see Richardson, *op. cit.*, pp. 108–110.

[13] *Reg. Romeyn*, I, 301.

[14] *Taxatio Ecclesiastica Angliae et Walliae Auctoritate P. Nicholai IV c. A.D. 1291* (London, 1802).

[15] Rose Graham, "The Taxation of Pope Nicholas," *English Historical Review*, 23 (1908), 434–454; Hartridge, *Vicarages*, p. 79.

[16] E. L. Cutts, *Parish Priests and Their People in the Middle Ages* (London, 1898).

[17] In order to be promoted to major orders a cleric had to show that he was capable of supporting himself from a benefice or otherwise. If he had private means he was said to be ordained "to the title of his own patrimony." H. S. Bennett, *The Pastons and Their England* (2d ed.; Cambridge, 1951), p. 214 n. 1, noted that 60 per cent of the Hereford ordinands were so ordained in the period 1328–1337. By 1378–1387 the proportion had fallen to 16 per cent. Similar figures are given in *Victoria County History, Warwickshire*, II, 16.

[18] C.16 q.1 c.66, X. 3.17.1. The decretal merely required parish priests to exhort their people to show hospitality, but the canonists took it as a basis for defining in detail the obligation of the laity to contribute to the support of the poor. See especially the comment of Hostiensis on this decretal: "It does not suffice to pay tithes in full unless alms are given from the nine parts." (*Commentaria ad* X. 3.17.1, fol. 57ᵛᵃ. Hostiensis made the same comment on X. 2.9.3, fol. 34ᵛᵃ.)

[19] *Wilkins*, II, 182. Pope Nicholas here followed the wording of a similar decree of Pope Gregory X issued in 1274. *Les Registres de Gregoire X*, ed. L. Auvray (Paris, 1892), p. 233.

[20] Richard Poore was successively bishop of Chichester (1215–1217), Salisbury (1217–1228), and Durham (1228–1237). His synodal statues were promulgated during the years 1217–1221. See C. R. Cheney, *English Synodalia of the Thirteenth Century* (Oxford, 1941), pp. 51–89.

[21] Gibbs and Lang, *op. cit.*, p. 117. Cheney points out that this work exaggerates the influence of Bishop Poore's statutes in the second half of the thirteenth century, but he agrees that the statutes were of great importance down to about 1240. *Synodalia*, p. 89.

[22] *Charters and Documents Illustrating the History . . . of Salisbury*, ed. W. R. Jones and W. D. Macray, Rolls Series, 97 (London, 1891), p. 135.

[23] *Wilkins*, I, 585.

[24] *Wilkins*, I, 659. On these statutes see Gibbs and Lang, *op. cit.*, p. 109.

[25] *Wilkins*, I, 672. There may be here an echo of Cicero, *De Officiis* 1.15.48, though indeed Cicero's comment tended in the opposite direction: "For if we do not

hesitate to confer benefits upon those who we hope will reward us in the future, how ought we to deal with those who have already helped us?"

[26] *Wilkins*, I, 673. On Walter de Cantilupe's statutes and their influence see Cheney, *Synodalia*, pp. 91–109.

[27] *Wilkins*, I, 691, 693. Cf. Cheney, *Synodalia*, pp. 84–89.

[28] *Wilkins*, I, 714; II, 147. Cf. Cheney, *Synodalia*, p. 49.

[29] *Wilkins*, II, 297: "Sanctione insuper praecipimus synodali quod de fructibus non residentium, quod tam de religiosis ecclesias parochiales in usus suos habentibus quam secularibus intelligi volumus, per nostram aut officialis nostri ordinationem, aliquae portiones in usus egentium parochianorum huiusmodi expendatur, non minus utique quam decima decimarum, illis autem religiosis exceptis qui ecclesias parochiales infra septa sui monasterii vel contiguas eidem monasterio habent." This statute was attributed by Wilkins to Bishop Herbert Woodloke, but see Cheney, *Synodalia*, pp. 103–108.

[30] W. H. Bliss, ed., *Calendar of Entries in the Papal Registers* . . . (London, 1893), p. 375.

[31] *Wilkins*, II, 57.

[32] *Reg. Quivil*, p. 321.

[33] *Wilkins*, II, 697.

[34] E. Brown, *Fasciculus Rerum Expetendarum* (London, 1690), II, 253.

[35] *Reg. Peckham*, I, 371.

[36] *Ibid.*, II, 670.

[37] *Ibid.*, II, 715; III, 827.

[38] *Ibid.*, III, 949.

[39] *Reg. Swinfield*, pp. 433, 455.

[40] J. E. Hirst, "Finances of the Dean and Chapter of Lincoln from the Twelfth to the Fourteenth Century," *Journal of Ecclesiastical History*, 5 (1954), 149–167. "The archdeacon took the farm [of the rectory of Glentham], agreeing to pay sixty marks yearly to the Common and being bound to spend five marks yearly *ad humanitatem faciendam in dicta parochia et ad ornamenta ecclesie*. The Common would, however, provide cloth, canvas and money for distribution as usual. The purchase of cloths of Candlewick Street and of cloths called *duddes* is of habitual occurrence in the accounts, for the gifts to poor parishioners of appropriated churches" (p. 161). The "Common" in this quotation is the fund held in common by the canons as distinct from their individual emoluments.

[41] Some examples are *Reg. Cantilupe*, pp. 7, 45, 168, 192, 217; *Reg. Gandavo*, II, 835, 843, 850; *Reg. Grandisson*, I, 338, 364, 369; *Reg. Kellawe*, I, 102, 139, 155; *Reg. Orletone*, p. 33; *Reg. Quivil*, pp. 313, 321.

[42] *Reg. Peckham*, II, 670.

[43] W. S. Simpson, ed., *Visitations of the Churches Belonging to St. Paul's Cathedral, 1249–52*, Camden Society, n.s. 55 (London, 1895); W. S. Simpson, ed., *Visitations of the Churches Belonging to St. Paul's Cathedral, 1297 and 1458*, vol. 9 of *Camden Miscellany* (London, 1895).

[44] *Reg. Winchelsey*, I, 1292.

[45] *Reg. Bronscombe*, p. 19.

[46] *Annales Monastici. Annales de Burton*, Rolls Series, 36 (London, 1864), p. 307. See Gibbs and Lang, *op. cit.*, pp. 160–161. St. Raymund de Pennaforte, in

his very influential *Summa de Penitentia* (*ca.* 1230), wrote that archdeacons visiting parishes were to inquire "whether [the priest] feeds his flock, assisting those who are in need and above all those who are sick. Works of mercy also are to be suggested by the archdeacon, to be done by him for their assistance. If he cannot fully accomplish them out of his own resources, he ought, according to his power, to use his personal influence to get from others the means of carrying them out. . . ." Cited by R. H. Tawney, *Religion and the Rise of Capitalism* (Pelican ed.; London, 1948), p. 290.

[47] *Reg. Grandisson*, I, 435.

[48] *Reg. Stapledon*, p. 130.

[49] *Reg. Stapledon*, pp. 57–58.

[50] G. G. Coulton, "A Visitation of the Archdeaconry of Totnes in 1342," *English Historical Review*, 26 (1911), 108–124, at p. 114. At Woton the parson was commended for having recently built a guesthouse (p. 118).

[51] *Reg. Kellawe*, IV, 412–413.

[52] *Reg. Peckham*, II, 479.

[53] *Matthaei Parisiensis . . . Chronica Majora*, ed. R. H. Luard, Rolls Series, 57 (7 vols.; London, 1872–1883), V, 405; trans. by J. A. Giles as *Matthew Paris's English History* (3 vols.; London, 1889–1893), III, 48.

[54] Luard, *op. cit.*, IV, 582–583; Giles, *op. cit.*, II, 193–194.

[55] Matthew Paris reported a similar protest by the rectors of Berkshire in 1240 (Luard, *op. cit.*, IV, 41; Giles, *op. cit.*, I, 285). In 1281 the clergy of the deanery of Holderness complained that rectors and vicars were being unduly burdened "while at the same time the number of poor people (to whom the goods of the church belong) is daily increasing" (*Reg. Wickwane*, pp. 248–249). In 1312 the English barons protested that a proposed papal tax would make it impossible for English benefices to continue to provide hospitality and alms, for which their endowments were intended (*Reg. Swinfield*, p. 472).

[56] *Reg. Newport*, p. 182.

CHAPTER VI: *The Later Middle Ages* (Pages 109–133)

[1] On these changes in the manorial economy see E. Lipson, *The Growth of English Society* (New York, 1953), pp. 15–21, or J. Clapham, *A Concise Economic History of Britain* (Cambridge, 1949), pp. 110–116. For more detailed discussions of the various problems involved see *The Cambridge Economic History*, Vol. I: *The Agrarian Life of the Middle Ages* (Cambridge, 1941).

[2] Josiah Cox Russel, *British Medieval Population* (Albuquerque, 1948).

[3] On these social repercussions of the Black Death see Clapham, *op. cit.*, pp. 116–124.

[4] There has been much discussion among economic historians concerning the causes and extent of the trade depression in the later Middle Ages. In assuming that there was a major falling off in trade and that the basic cause of this was the decline in population after the Black Death, I have followed the views of M. M. Postan in *The Cambridge Economic History*, Vol. II: *Trade and Industry in the Middle Ages* (Cambridge, 1952), pp. 191–215.

[5] M. W. Beresford, *The Lost Villages of England* (New York, 1954).

[6] W. Ferguson, "The Church in a Changing World," *American Historical Re-*

view, 59 (1953), 1–18. This article discusses perceptively the reaction of the Papacy to the changing economic environment of the later Middle Ages. For the effect of Urban V's decree on appropriation of parish churches in England, see K. L. Wood-Legh, *Studies in Church Life in England under Edward III* (Cambridge, 1934), pp. 133–134: "The decree certainly delayed many appropriations, but its success in lessening the number that were eventually appropriated may be questioned. For almost as soon as it had been published, the pope began to receive petitions to allow particular appropriations to be carried out, in spite of the general prohibition, and these petitions were seldom refused." Indeed, a more vicious form of appropriation appeared in the late fourteenth century. Hitherto parish churches had been appropriated and vicars appointed instead of parsons. Now the better-endowed vicarages were themselves appropriated. See Hartridge, *Vicarages*, pp. 182 ff.

[7] See Susan Wood, *English Monasteries and Their Patrons in the Thirteenth Century* (Oxford, 1955), pp. 138–139.

[8] H. S. Bennett, *The Pastons and Their England* (2d ed.; Cambridge, 1951), p. 214 n. 1; *Victoria County History, Warwickshire*, II, 16.

[9] For a general discussion on this theme, with elaborate bibliography, see Benjamin N. Nelson, *The Idea of Usury. From Tribal Brotherhood to Universal Otherhood* (Princeton, 1949). One of the canonistic controversies on usury did have some direct bearing on the welfare of the poor, the controversy concerning the licitness of the *monti di pietà*. These were a kind of pawnshop, established with ecclesiastical approval, and they had exactly the same purpose as credit unions in modern society, to provide people of modest means with small loans and so save them from the necessity of resorting to usurers. See *ibid.*, pp. 19–20.

[10] Joannes de Turrecremata, *Repertorium ad Dist.*86, I, fols. 253^r–260^r.

[11] This remained a commonplace of medieval preaching and teaching. For typical fifteenth-century canonistic discussions see Panormitanus, *Commentaria ad X.* 3.5.10, VI, fol. 42^r; Joannes de Turrecremata, *Repertorium ad Dist.*47 c.8, I, fol. 176; Dominicus de Sancto Gemignano, *Commentaria ad Dist.*47 c.8, fol. 106ra.

[12] Panormitanus, *Commentaria ad X.* 2.20.8, IV, fol. 64va; Lanfrancus de Oriano, *Repetitiones*, III, fol. 260ra; Joannes de Turrecremata, *Repertorium ad C.*2 q.1 c.4, II, fol. 60va.

[13] Antonius de Burgos, *Repetitiones*, IV, fol. 252^r; Stephanus de Gaeta, *Repetitiones*, I, fol. 193^r; Joannes de Turrecremata, *Repertorium ad Dist.*47 c.8, I, fols. 176va–177ra (a particularly nuanced discussion); *ad Dist.*86 c.19, I, fols. 258rb–259va; *ad Dist.*86 c.21, I, fol. 259^v; Panormitanus, *Commentaria ad X.* 2.24.8, IV, fol. 198va; Dominicus de Sancto Gemignano, *Commentaria ad Dist.*47 c.8, fol. 107va.

[14] Panormitanus, for instance, closely followed the views of Innocent IV in his *Commentaria ad X.* 1.29.38, II, fols. 153vb–154ra. See also his remarks at X. 2.2.11, III, fol. 103vb, X. 2.2.15, III, fol. 118vb, X. 3.17.1, VI, fol. 130va. Joannes de Turrecremata, on the other hand, thought that Innocent's claims were too sweeping and preferred the view of Bernardus Parmensis that cases of widows and other "wretched persons" belonged "principally and primarily" to the secular courts and fell under the jurisdiction of the Church only when the secular judge had been negligent. *Repertorium ad Dist.*87 c.1, I, fol. 261va.

15 Joannes de Turrecremata, *Repertorium ad* C.11 q.3 c.72, II, fol. 196rb; Felinus de Sandeus, *Commentaria ad* X. 2.20.8; Joannes de Nigris, *Repetitiones*, VI, fol. 8vb.

16 Panormitanus, *Commentaria ad* X. 3.17.1, VI, fol. 130; Antonius de Burgos, *Repetitiones*, IV, fol. 252r.

17 Panormitanus, *Commentaria ad* X. 3.5.12, VI, fol. 43vb. He added, however, that if a poor man was actually starving his needs took precedence over all other claims on the church: "Non enim tenentur omnes recipere, et postea mendicare, sed primo subveniendum est servitoribus. . . . Item reparanda est prius ecclesia . . . et ex aliis redditibus poterit teneri hospitalitas . . . et intellige nisi tanta sit necessitas proximi, quam fame moreretur, nam tunc ecclesia tenetur etiam vendere bona mobilia, et immobilia, et etiam vasa ecclesiae. . . ." See also his *Commentaria ad* X. 3.48.4, VI, fol. 339rb.

18 E.g., Joannes de Turrecremata, *Repertorium ad Dist.*42 c.2, I, fol. 162rb; ad *Dist.*86 c.14, I, fol. 255v; Stephanus de Gaeta, *Repetitiones*, I, fol. 193rb; Dominicus de Sancto Gemignano, *Commentaria ad Dist.*42 c.2, fol. 97rb–va (citing from Guido de Baysio the distinction between "day-to-day alms" and "premeditated alms"); Panormitanus, *Commentaria ad* X. 2.28.53, V, fol. 185rb.

19 *Repertorium ad Dist.*82 c.1, I, fol. 245va.

20 *Repertorium ad Dist.*86 c.14, I, fol. 255r, and ad *Dist.*86 c.19, I, fol. 259r. See pp. 56–57, above.

21 *Commentaria*, VIII, 76 (Consilium 55): "Et circa hoc advertendum quod civilia iura et canonica expresse reprobant mendicitatem publicam sine evidenti causa necessitatis, ut 1. unica C. de mendi vali. lib. 2 [Code 11.26.1] et 93 dist. c. diaconi § Nunc autem iuncta glossa et c. seq. Sed si nulla necessitas est, cum possent victum manibus quaerere, et non tollere pauperum indigentium subsidia, ergo eorum status est ab utroque iure improbatus."

22 John of Ayton *ad Constitutiones Legatinae* in *Provinciale*, p. 96. See the decrees of Archbishop Peckham and Archbishop Stratford cited above, pages 100–101.

23 After a distinguished career in the Church and in the king's service, Lyndwood became Bishop of St. Davids in 1442. He died in 1446.

24 *Provinciale*, p. 68, Gloss s.v. *Ad pauperes audiendos.*

25 *Provinciale*, p. 67, Gloss s.v. *Eleemosynarios.*

26 *Provinciale*, p. 133, Gloss s.v. *Necessitati extremae.* See above, p. 36.

27 *Provinciale*, p. 67, Gloss s.v. *Hospitales.*

28 This could have been taken to mean that rectors who did have vicars were themselves free from any obligation to keep hospitality. Lyndwood discussed the point but rejected this interpretation because the general rule of canon law required all priests and prelates to be hospitable. *Provinciale*, p. 132, Gloss s.v. *Nec habent vicarios.*

29 *Provinciale*, p. 133, Gloss s.v. *Eleemosynae.*

30 *Provinciale*, p. 152, Gloss s.v. *Pinguis portio:* "Secundum facultates ecclesiae et considerata qualitate et indigentia personae locantis. . . . Debet etiam considerari numerus et indigentia huiusmodi pauperum. . . ." For the various numerical estimates of the proper portion to be assigned to the poor see *Provinciale*, p. 134, Gloss s.v. *Arbitrio*, and p. 152, Gloss s.v. *Jura consona.*

31 Gasquet, *Parish Life*, p. 84. Lyndwood's comment is at page 133 of the *Provinciale*, s.v. *Hospitalitatis.*

32 Coulton, *Five Centuries*, III, 203, 650–651.

33 N. Didier, "Henri de Suse en Angleterre (?1236–1244)," *Studi Arangio-Ruiz* (Naples, 1952), II, 335–351, and "Henri de Suse, Évêque de Sisteron (1244–1250)," *Nouvelle Revue de Droit Français et Étranger*, 31 (1953), 244–270, 409–429. On the activities of Hostiensis in England see F. M. Powicke, *King Henry III and the Lord Edward* (Oxford, 1947), I, 272–273.

34 Joannes Andreae, *Novella ad Decretales*, 3.5.16. The words of Hostiensis himself were: ". . . nam et in provincia minus beneficium potest assignari quia minores expensas requirit quam in Anglia quae maiores expensas facere consuevit, et si de personis aequalibus agatur." (*Commentaria ad X.* 3.5.16.)

35 *Provinciale*, p. 134, Gloss s.v. *Arbitrio:* "Tertio quaero, nunquid facta moderatione hujus summae per episcopum, oriatur ex hoc istis pauperibus aliqua actio? Videtur quod non, quia cum personae istorum pauperum sint incertae, non potest constare, quibus eorum applicetur obligatio, quae est mater actionis personalis. . . . Puto tamen quod si in parochia esset collegium pauperum, quod tunc eis tanquam personae satis certae daretur actio. Si non sit collegium, tunc sicut alias favore pietatis valet relictum pauperibus licet personis incertis. . . . Posset dici quod eis etiam competat actio ex favore, cum pauperes in casu nostro certi sint, videlicet unius certae parochiae. . . . Securius tamen est, quod eis per officium iudicis, quod actioni deservit, sucurratur, vel per episcopum qui est in hoc casu isporum procurator legitimus. . . ." On this passage see Coulton, *Five Centuries*, III, 205–206. His comments again seem based on a series of misunderstandings of the canonistic doctrines involved.

36 It was often held by the canonists that the inmates of a hospital constituted a corporate group in whom the legal rights of the institution inhered. See Jean Imbert, *Les hôpitaux en droit canonique* (Paris, 1947), p. 112.

37 In the fragment that has been printed from the court book of Lyndwood's contemporary, Bishop Alnwick of Lincoln, there are two cases of parish rectors cited before the bishop's court on charges that included failure to keep hospitality. See A. Hamilton Thompson, *The English Clergy and Their Organization in the Later Middle Ages* (Oxford, 1947), pp. 232, 236.

38 Cited in "Anglo-Norman Canonists," *Traditio*, VII (1949–1951), 352.

39 *Glossa Palatina ad Dist.*47 c.8 (citing Huguccio), MS Pal.Lat.658, fol. 12rb. The view of Alanus was mentioned by Bernardus Parmensis, *Gl. Ord. ad* X. 3.17.1, and by Innocent IV, *Commentaria ad X.* 3.17.1, p. 468.

40 *Gl. Ord. ad* X. 3.17.1.

41 *Commentaria ad* X. 3.17.1, p. 468.

42 *Commentaria ad* X. 3.17.1, fol. 57va. Hostiensis also suggested another interpretation of the text: "Thus the sense is that priests ought to be hospitable for they can even be compelled to this by excommunication, . . . but the laity cannot be compelled to this, and so what is said here about hospitality refers to clerics only and what is said about selling refers to lay folk only."

43 *Gl. Ord. ad Extrav. Jo. XXII*, 1.3.1. Zenzellinus' gloss is cited in chap. iv, n. 22, above. He did not present the position of Hostiensis quite accurately.

44 *Distinctiones ad* X. 3.17.1, p. 430.

45 *Commentaria ad* X. 3.17.1, fol. 56vb.

46 Stephanus de Gaeta, *Repetitiones*, I, fol. 193rb: "Finally note that a poor man can implore the office of the bishop to compel a rich man to give alms." Panormi-

tanus, *Commentaria ad* X. 3.17.1, VI, fol. 130: "Although no action belongs to the needy against the rich, . . . nevertheless they can implore the office of superiors that they may compel them [to give]. . . . Innocent seems to hold the contrary unless the sin is notorious. I distinguish. Either one speaks of a beneficed cleric or a layman. In the first case he can be compelled to be charitable according to his resources. . . . In the second case, when it is a question of laymen, I say that where there is very great need on the part of a neighbor, a layman sins in not helping him, and so can be compelled to help by excommunication." The views of Felinus de Sandeus and of Dominicus de Sancto Gemignano were cited by Antonius de Burgos. See n. 47.

[47] *Repetitiones*, IV, fol. 252^r: "The second conclusion is that laymen can be compelled by the office of the judge to give alms. . . . Concerning [this] second conclusion, which refers to laymen, the theory is common to the writers everywhere as you can see from Abbas [Panormitanus] and Dominicus de Sancto Gemignano and Felinus Sandeus. . . ." The phrases "implore the office of the judge" or "implore the office of the bishop" commonly used by the canonists in these discussions were technical terms used in the initiation of a suit by the process of *denunciatio evangelica.*

[48] "Aequitas canonica ed equity inglese alla luce del pensiero di C. Saint Germain," *Ephemerides Iuris Canonici*, 3 (1947), 3–23, and, especially, H. Coing, "English Equity and the *Denunciatio Evangelica* of the Canon Law," *Law Quarterly Review*, 71 (1955), 223–241.

[49] 5 and 6 Edward VI, c. 2. Cited by J. R. Tanner, *Tudor Constitutional Documents* (2d ed.; Cambridge, 1948), p. 471.

[50] Hartridge, *Vicarages*, p. 159; Coulton, *Five Centuries*, III, 210.

[51] A. E. Bland, P. A. Brown, and R. H. Tawney, *English Economic History. Selected Documents* (London, 1930), pp. 164–167.

[52] 12 Richard II, c.7; Bland, Brown, and Tawney, *op. cit.*, p. 174. "Further, it is agreed and assented that touching every man who goes begging and is able to serve or labour, it be done with him as with him who departs out of hundreds and other places aforesaid without a letter testimonial. . . . And that beggars unable to serve remain in the cities and towns where they are dwelling at the time of the proclamation of this statute; and that if the people of the said cities or towns will not or cannot suffice to find them, the said beggars withdraw to the other towns within the hundred, rape or wapentake, or to the towns where they were born, within forty days after the said proclamation be made, and dwell there continually for their lives."

[53] 15 Richard II, c. 6. Cited by Hartridge, *Vicarages*, p. 157. On the enforcement of this act see Coulton, *Five Centuries*, III, 209.

[54] Bernardus Parmensis, Innocent IV, Hostiensis, *ad* X. 4.8.1.

[55] 22 Henry VIII, c. 12; Tanner, *op. cit.*, pp. 475–479.

[56] 27 Henry VIII, c. 25; Tanner, *op. cit.*, pp. 479–481.

[57] 5 Elizabeth I, c. 3; Tanner, *op. cit.*, pp. 471–472.

[58] S. L. Ware, *The Elizabethan Parish in Its Ecclesiastical and Financial Aspects* (Baltimore, 1908). Cf. Webb, *Poor Law History*, I, 8 n. 1.

Index

Index